Communication

Team

nsley

2004

Published by Stephen Hancocks Limited
27 Bellamy's Court, Abbotshade Road,
London SE16 5RF

ISBN 095461451 8

Printed and bound by Dennis Barber Limited. Lowestoft, Suffolk

Preface

The provision of dental care is undergoing perhaps the most profound change it has ever faced. With the loss of fee-for-item of service National Health Service dentistry and the advent of the new oral health assessment, the concept of team work will increase and the roles and responsibilities of the members of the team will change dramatically. These changes will undoubtedly bring new and exciting challenges to all team members. Whilst, as yet, the precise format of care provision remains a little unclear, what is certain is that the team's ability to communicate, both with patients and with each other will grow hugely in importance. For these reasons, we felt it imperative to develop a revised edition of *Communication and the Dental Team*. The first edition was hugely popular and, we are told, much enjoyed, yet feedback from participants at lectures and conferences has suggested that a new book would be welcomed – but would need to be more easily available and accessible. We have worked hard with our publisher, Stephen Hancocks, to try to meet the needs which have been communicated to us. And so here it is, an updated, modernised version of "Communication" which we hope will encourage and develop all members to enable them to have rapport with patients as a central concept in their practices. Using the techniques and skills we describe in this book will help dentists, professions complementary to dentistry and all team members.

The book is designed to help the team to place the patient at the heart of dental practice and to allow patients to participate fully in their care. Care of clients in any successful organisation begins and ends with communication. Dental care is no different. Our observation is that the teams in happy, successful dental practices smile and talk a lot. This book is intended to bring that ambience to all practices.

Elizabeth Kay
Stella Tinsley
October 2004

Contents

Relationships with Patients - Why Bother?

Introduction

Think about why you chose dentistry as a career? Although the money, status and, best of all, the uniforms and white coats were all appealing, most people chose to be involved in dentistry because they wanted a job which deals with people, and even perhaps because they wanted to feel that they could help others. Dentistry is to do with relationships with people, although unfortunately it is all too easy to forget that there is actually a real live person (that is, a complex mass of personality, feelings, priorities, lifestyle, etc., etc.) attached to a tooth, especially when you are immersed in a complex, physically and mentally demanding technical task. Yet sadly, or perhaps realistically, it is documented that dental students change as they go through their undergraduate courses, from people who entered dentistry as people-centred, caring beings, to individuals whose priorities are the mechanical and technical aspects of tooth restoration and, of course, money[1]!

The importance of interpersonal skills, as well as technical skills, was officially recognised in the UK in 1989 when the General Dental Council stated that the teaching of behavioural sciences ought to become a mandatory part of dental training. Now enshrined in the GDC's curriculum document *The First Five Years*[2], this recognition implies that, if we are already 'good with people', we can develop and improve these skills and, if we are not the type of person who intuitively 'gets on' easily with people, then it is possible to **learn** to do so. Since most successful, happy dental teams claim that it is their relationships with their patients, which makes their chosen career enjoyable, then surely the skills of relating well to patients are ones which are worth acquiring or improving? It is our view that it is extremely difficult to make an important contribution to a **'good'** dental practice without these skills. They are skills that can be learnt and developed with practice, exactly like skills with a high-speed turbine or dental materials. And, just as technical competence grows and you become more confident when using the requisite dexterous skills every day, communication skills can also be fostered and developed through practice and constant use.

It is not possible to truly 'help' and 'care' for patients in a way that will cause them to trust, and have high regard for you, without good interpersonal skills. It is by your communication with your patients that they judge you. The dentist's (unquestionable!) ability at spotting incipient decay, the hygienist's brilliance at removing every last vestige of calculus from a sub-gingival pocket, or the nurse's dexterity with spatula and alginate have almost **nothing** to do with whether or not patients decide that the team is competent and able to look after their mouths well. They cannot see these things, do not know the importance of them, and, for the most part could not care less anyway. This is not to say that technical skills are not of great importance - merely that those are not the skills by which patients choose or judge the people who care for their teeth and mouths. If you listened to a group of individuals discussing the merits or otherwise of the dental practice they attend, it is doubtful that they would be heard to exclaim:

"ooh, that dental nurse never picks the right matrix band"

"do you know, the therapist provided an adrenaline-free local anaesthetic to my medically compromised daughter with out a second thought?"

"the receptionist is a complete whiz at scheduling appointments with Superdent Time Wizard™"

And do people, when suggesting a particular practice to a friend, illustrate their dentist's skills by lifting their lip to expose the astounding accuracy of their crown margins? Of course they don't. They would be more likely to talk about the convenience of the practice and the ease of parking, the smell of coffee when they enter the building. Most importantly, they would describe how they felt about the way they had been treated, as a person:

"The nurses are brilliant, so friendly, and they always remember you."
"He's really chatty - never feels like he's rushing me out."
"She feels more like a friend than a hygienist."

The purpose of this book is, firstly, to try to explain, using both research findings and the anecdotal experience of one dentist and one patient, why communication skills and the relationships between the dental team and the patient are important. Secondly, the book aims to show how, in practical terms, the skill required to develop these relationships can be improved and developed.

Why do we need to relate well to patients?

Relating well with patients, quite apart from any other advantages that it confers upon the practice in which you work, enables you to get appropriate information from the patient quickly and easily. The more skilled the dental team, the less difficulty the patient will find in describing or explaining their problem. So, establishing a good rapport with a patient at the outset will enable you to define the patient's problem and determine an appropriate solution rapidly. And they'll like that because they'll believe that you care, as indeed you do. Approximately 80 per cent of the information we need in order to make a diagnosis comes from the 'chat' which precedes examination. (Practices often like to call this part of a visit a consultation, but to the patient it is a chat about himself or herself). Thus, skills in non-verbal and verbal communication enable a dental practice to bypass irrelevant information and to quickly pinpoint the most important issues and facts, without offending the patient, or appearing to be disinterested.

The third reason for needing to be competent in interpersonal relationships with patients is that, at some point, it is likely that we are going to have to explain the nature and cause of the patient's oral ill-health, advise them about the treatment options available, make clear to them what we plan to do and have them recognise their own role in the treatment. Finally, it will be necessary to both explain why we are suggesting one particular option as the best course of action **and** ask them to pay for their treatment. **Most** importantly (remembering that the actions and behaviours a person undertakes on a day to day basis, at home, will have infinitely more effect on their ultimate oral health than anything we may do in the surgery) we will need to let the patient understand what they need to do to help them deal with their problem on their own.

Finally, a good relationship between health care personnel and the recipient of care has a powerful therapeutic effect. For example, it has been demonstrated that 64 per cent of patients suffering from pain, clicking and limitation of movement of their temporomandibular joints will report a noticeable improvement in their symptoms when their only 'treatment' has been an explanation about the nature of their disease and enthusiastic reassurance that their symptoms will subside. So, a good relationship with patients can actually make them feel healthier!

What exactly are we trying to achieve?

> The first stage of a dental consultation is to determine the nature of the patient's problem in physical and social and psychological terms.

Most patients attend a dental surgery because they either have a problem, which they believe to be related to their oral health, or because they wish to avoid certain events that they would regard as a problem, for example, loss of teeth or toothache. Those who do not regard the loss of teeth as a problem tend not to attend for dental care. Suggesting that 'defining the problem' is a good first step is not the same as saying that the best thing to tell the patient is what disease, or pathology, is present in her or his mouth. The 'disease' is **not** the same as the patient's perception of a problem (or potential problem).

It **may** be that the patient has attended because they have toothache - in that case, the problem **is** a physical one. However, what of the patient who claims that they are attending because their gums bleed? Often, the bleeding has been present, perhaps only intermittently, for many years. Perhaps their real 'problem' (as opposed to their 'complaint') is that they fear they have bad breath. In this case, their problem may be socially rooted (they have no friends and rather than admit that it is their habits and behaviour which make them unpopular, wish to blame their lack of social life on their unpleasant breath).

Worse, someone may have confided to them that they smell unpleasant. Such a devastating revelation would be highly likely to trigger a dental visit. Informing such a patient that they have 'periodontal disease and marginal gingivitis', although it may make the dental team marvel at their own fabulous diagnostic powers, will do **nothing** towards solving the problem. Such a patient will then merely have the added worry of a terrifying-sounding disease alongside their social unacceptability.

A further example of the psycho-social, rather than pathological nature of oral 'problems', would be the burning mouth syndrome patient. Many patients who report an intense burning sensation in their mouths are actually terrified of oral cancer or other terminal or incurable diseases. Exactly why such worries are translated into oral symptoms is not known, but many such patients will repeatedly visit various dental and medical practitioners with their complaint, until someone recognises the psychological cause of the symptoms. 'Chopping' a piece of tissue out of the patient's mouth in order for it to be viewed under a microscope will make the problem worse, rather than better.

And what of the patient who attends the dental surgery, saying that their teeth are wearing away because they grind them at night? Is that person's problem really the loss of tooth tissue, or is the real problem that they wish to share, the stress that is causing the grinding and clenching. Or, perhaps, it is simply that their partner is moaning about the grinding noise at night? It is vital that the dental care professional determines the **true** nature of the 'problem' before embarking upon lengthy, complicated and expensive procedures to 'treat' it. If the dentist has wrongly diagnosed that the patient's concern is the appearance of worn teeth and complex treatment is undertaken to solve the tooth wear, it will actually do little to alleviate the true problem (the grumbling moaning partner) – in fact it might make it worse by adding to the patient's worries about how to explain the large bill to the sleep deprived partner.

> The second stage of a dental consultation is to communicate your understanding of the problem to the patient.

Unfortunately, recognition of the patient's perception of the problem is not enough. Patients are not psychic. Unless the dental team communicates its understanding to the patient, the patient will remain unaware that the dental practice recognise anything other than oral disease. Imagine the patient who says to the receptionist: "I hear the dentist has just been on a course about implants". Would it be helpful in this situation for the receptionist to say: "Yeah, it's great, we can now do operations where we drill a bit of metal into the gum to hold false teeth in place"?

It is vital that the receptionist picks up that the patient is interested, and perhaps not unworried that the dentist has just acquired a new technique, which he may want to practise on his patients. A more useful response would be to express back to the patient the understanding that the news is of concern, and reassure the worried individual that this does not mean that the dentist will, from now on, be treating his patients differently! For example:

Patient: *"I hear the dentist has just been on a course about implants."*

Receptionist: *"Yes she has, but it won't affect your treatment. It's only used on very difficult cases".*

Patients do not know that their worries, concerns and problems, and the impact that these have on their lives, have been understood, unless someone communicates that understanding to them.

However, equally, it is may be that the patient has heard, or read, about the success of implants in improving quality of life but is conscious of seeming to be too vain in asking directly about them. Here a dental team member with a sensitivity to the patient's motive might answer the same point:

"Yes. Implants can make such a positive difference to people's lives nowadays and we wanted to be able to offer the benefits to our patients too. Would you like to know more about how they could help you?"

The third step in a dental consultation is to decide upon the best treatment option - taking into account the patient's social circumstances.

Once a member of the dental team (often this will **not** be the dentist) has recognised the true nature of the patient's problem, and have communicated their views on, and understanding of, the problem to the patient, the dentist must then, using his/her professional knowledge and skills, decide upon a course of action which is the most appropriate. This will be dictated not only by the problem, but also by the attitudes, beliefs, wishes and lifestyle of the patient. For example, it might be inappropriate to decide upon a six-visit programme for full mouth restorations, if the patient happens to be the mother of five toddlers, who lives thirty miles from the practice and does not possess a car. Thus, the life-circumstances of each patient will and should influence which treatment option is chosen as offering the best solution to the problem. The preferred 'technical solution' may not be the best solution if the patient is considered as a person rather than a biomechanical problem.

The fourth stage of the consultation is to involve the patient in the decision about the best solution to the problem.

Having suggested one, two or possibly more viable options aimed at solving the patient's problems (not just his or her disease), it is vital that they then have some degree of control over the decision. Patients should ideally choose what is to be the course of action and be fully aware of the possible outcomes. Involvement of patients at this stage is the key to their satisfaction with the treatment provided. If a treatment plan includes root-treating and crowning three teeth, the patient needs to understand the length of time required for such treatment. He will then have to make a decision as to whether he can afford the time and the expense involved. The team must also ensure that the patient fully recognises the home after-care that the patient's mouth will then require. There are often cases where a seemingly 'sub-optimal' treatment plan is actually the one that offers the patient the most acceptable solution to the problem.

The importance of this shared responsibility for the outcome of treatment cannot be overemphasised. Dentists are not gods or goddesses and do not, on their own, hold all the solutions to all their patients' problems. If they are acting together, the dental team and the patient have a much greater chance of a satisfactory outcome and this partnership approach, rather than 'us-and-them', approach has a variety of other benefits which we will attempt to explain in greater detail in later chapters. Suffice it to say that it can be an immense relief to drop the omnipotent 'healer' role and develop joint responsibility with patients. Despite many advances in oral health care, we still do not have all the answers and, therefore, really should not pretend that we have. While we sometimes have the 'right' solutions in the 'scientific' sense and while we undoubtedly bring a wealth of knowledge and expertise to our patients, it is desperately important to remember that so do the patients. Just because the team's information is based on clinical science, this does not mean that it is any 'better' than the patient's views, which are founded on their own personal experiences and the ideas prevalent in their social group. Because you are right in science, does not mean you are necessarily 'right' in the patient's eyes.

> What does he mean: no such thing as weak teeth! Granny had them,
> Mum's got them. The man's a fool.

Last thoughts

Many studies have shown that patients understand, accept and act upon the information given to them by health care professionals if the health professional's view is consistent with their own beliefs and personal explanations of health and disease. Therefore, the members of a dental practice ignore their patients' perceptions at their peril. Unless the dental team elicits and understands the beliefs of the patient, the patient is unlikely to heed or understand the views of the professionals. The patient's interpretation of her or his symptoms and problems has validity and authority in their own lives and social circles, even if it does **not** accord with the professional interpretations of health and disease. It is perhaps wise to remember that 'science' has got things wrong in the past (vis a vis "calcium builds strong bones and teeth", "eating raw vegetables gives you healthy gums", both of which have been used in dental health campaigns). Equally, tincture of foxglove **is** actually digitalis (digoxin) and really **did/does** help heart failure, even though it was thought of as an old wives' tale.

References

1. Kress GC. The impact of professional education on the performance of dentists. *Social Science and Dentistry*, Vol. II. London; FDI, 1985
2. *The First Five Years*. London; General Dental Council, 2002.

Further reading

Mataki S. Patient-dentist relationship. *J Med Dent Sci* 2000 **47:** 209-241.

Newsome P R. Current issues in dental practice management. Part 3. Attracting and keeping patients. *Prim Dent Care* 2003 **10:** 109-112.

Stahl B. Foundations of a trusting doctor–patient relationship. *Quint Int* 2003 **34:** 85-86.

Whitehouse J. Missed opportunities. Patients lost due to lack of understanding and marketing. *Dent Today* 2003 **22:** 112-117.

First Impressions

2

"O wad some Pow'r the giftie gie us
To see oursels as others see us
It wad frae mony a blunder free us
And foolish notion"

R Burns

Introduction

Consider a person's first visit to a dental practice. How did they come to decide to visit the dentist? Having taken that decision, why have they chosen this one particular practice? And, having experienced a visit to that surgery, will they be happy to return for further visits?

If a practice (as opposed to a practitioner) is to relate well to both patients (and perhaps even more importantly) to potential patients, these are important questions. It is well known that many people who have high levels of oral disease, and even discomfort, often choose **not** to visit a dental surgery. On the other hand, there are also some patients who have no disease, who attend as regularly as clockwork. If a dental practice is to attract patients who are satisfied, regularly attending and loyal, the dental team need to know the reasons why people do, and do not, attend for care. Equally, a dental team who know about the factors that make patients satisfied or unsatisfied with the treatment they receive can be an extremely powerful practice marketing tool. Listed below are four factors that will affect whether or not someone will attend a dental practice (or take some other action) in order to avoid the consequences of oral disease.

(1) Do people know about the diseases in their mouth?

If a person is going to even think about obtaining dental care, then they must have sufficient information available to them. They need to know about the diseases that can affect the mouth and must be able to recognise the signs and symptoms of disease. If they are to undertake 'preventive' dental behaviours, they also need to know what causes oral disease. Unless they have this knowledge, how can they possibly be expected to even consider the concept of visiting a 'mouth specialist'?

Dental professionals often make the mistake of assuming that they are the only ones who pass on information about oral health to the population at large. However, everyone has a 'dental career' long before, and quite separate from, any contact with a dentist or hygienist or any other member of the dental team. That is, people come across 'dental issues' through their friends, their family, their peer group and especially through the very powerful medium of television. Everyone has made decisions (consciously or unconsciously) about their mouth and those choices (for example, whether or not to brush their teeth each day) are made without any 'help' from dental personnel. Such decisions are part of everyday life and are related to the person's overall lifestyle. For example, in the UK, the majority of people know that sweet foods cause tooth decay; many know that brushing their teeth prevents gum disease and the majority will say, when asked, that visiting the dentist is important for the maintenance of dental health. However, since many people do not take up these actions, it is clear that knowing about habits which are conducive to oral health is a totally insufficient basis for prompting action.

So, knowledge about oral health threats are required if people are to take action for the maintenance of their mouth, BUT, such information usually comes from a person's immediate everyday surroundings, not the dental team. On its own, knowledge is an insufficient prompt to action.

(2) Will it happen to me?

A further requirement if people are to take action (for example, attend the dentist) for the sake of their oral health, is that they must perceive themselves to be susceptible to disease. Say, for example, you knew that your teeth were definitely going to fall out if you did not attend for regular dental visits - then you might be tempted to take action! However, the human race seems to have a quite remarkable sense of 'it won't happen to me'. Thus, even though people know about a disease and are aware that they have a fairly high probability of getting that disease, they will consider themselves to be 'the exception which proves the rule' and will believe that although everyone else who behaves like them will get the disease, they personally will escape. The skilled chest physician who smokes and who isn't deterred from the habit by his knowledge of lung cancer is a prime example of this sense of 'it may get everyone else, but it won't get me'. This feeling of invulnerability is perhaps one of the reasons why many people never bother to attend for dental care.

So, besides needing to know about oral disease, people also need to feel that these diseases are personally relevant before they will take action.

(3) "So what, if I've got rotten teeth and gums!?"

What of the people who know the symptoms of disease and recognise them in themselves but still do not take action? Why does someone in that position fail to do anything which would improve their lot? It seems that in order to prompt a visit to the dentist, patients must not only have knowledge about the disease and must believe themselves to be susceptible: in addition they need to feel that the disease will affect their lives in some important way. As an example, imagine a teenager who does not brush his teeth and who recognises that he has the symptoms of gingivitis. He may do nothing about his gums until his true love refuses to kiss him. At this point, the condition begins to impinge on the teenager's life in a way that is important to him. Action is triggered and he will take steps to rectify the situation in order that his sex life may continue unimpeded! Therefore, it seems that unless people recognise that they are susceptible to a condition that will seriously affect their life in some way, they will not take action.

(4) It's not worth it

Finally, there are people who recognise that they have a condition, e.g. they have spotted some decay in their teeth, so are sure they have a problem. They are also suffering toothache that is preventing them from doing the things they usually do. That is, they have appropriate information, they feel that the disease is personally relevant, and it is affecting their life in some way. What on earth would prevent a person in such a position from obtaining dental care? The answer lies in costs and benefits. A trip to the dentist is perceived as costly not only in terms of money, but also in terms of time, anguish, worry, time off work, travelling and so forth. Unless the person believes that the 'pay off' (reduction in symptoms) is worth the effort (time, money, etc.) and that the improvement she will get will be sufficient to warrant all the hassle, she will tend to try to ignore the symptoms. This is important, because it means that the degree of faith that a person has in their dentist's abilities will affect the point at which they feel that a trip to the dentist is worthwhile. If the dentist 'might' make them better, they are less likely to attend than if they believe that the dentist will definitely make them better.

Visiting the dentist - The Health Belief Model

Caries, what's caries? (KNOWLEDGE)
It might get him, but it won't get me! (PERCEIVED SUSCEPTIBILITY)
So what, who cares about tooth decay? (PERCEIVED SEVERITY)
It's not worth the effort (PERCEIVED COSTS + BENEFITS)

Having made the decision to go, how can a patient tell which surgery is best?

Given that there is a point at which most patients will seek help - whether this is a mother seeking preventive care for a disease-free toddler, or a person in screaming agony seeking relief from toothache - how do they decide which dental surgery to go to?

Advertising

It is worthwhile mentioning advertisements since, perhaps surprisingly, it has only been legal for dentists to advertise their practices since 1988. Therefore, the profession as a whole is relatively inexperienced with this particular method of marketing a practice. The great majority of dentists are listed in the 'Yellow Pages' and this could be construed as advertising their practice, although many more bizarre marketing strategies have been tried (for example, stickers on city centre rubbish bins!). Some dentists place notices in local newspapers, arrange leaflet drops, advertise in restaurants or appear in local brochures. The question is, do such techniques make any difference to the numbers and types of patients who attend a given practice? Most dentists who advertise would dispute that it does. Dentists in practice generally agree that the best form of advertising that a practice can have is recommendation by patients - and once again, one must remember that this recommendation will not be based on the perfection of the dentistry carried out, but on how the patient **feels** when they leave the practice. It has been said that a person who is dissatisfied with the treatment they have received will tell eleven people, a person who is satisfied will tell no one. Only if patients are delighted with their experience at the surgery will they report to others. On average, each of these people will tell three others about the surgery they have attended. It is clear then that making people happy is well worthwhile, but not necessarily easy to do.

Advertisements may be useful for informing people about practice arrangements, opening times, etc. but research has shown that few people, other than established, regularly-attending patients, or those in desperate need, notice such ads. Any form of advertisement is therefore noticed most by those who already go to a dentist, or are about to go, out of necessity. Consequently, advertising tends only to attract the eye of symptomatic attenders (emergency patients). It is possible that a practice might increase its patient pool by first attracting such patients via advertisement, then marketing themselves once the person has attended, but in general, advertising appears to do little to expand a practice's clientele. Despite this, many dentists spend significant amounts of money on advertising, often simply because other practices in the area advertise.

Telephone calls

The first contact

Imagine you are an anxious patient who for weeks has been plucking up the courage to make a dental appointment. You have asked your friends and they have suggested a particular surgery. You have been given the number and eventually you go to the telephone and dial. The type of response on the other end of the telephone will play a large part in:

(a) your decision to make an appointment

(b) the likelihood of you keeping that appointment

(c) how you feel when you get to the practice

(d) how you react to the practice as a whole

(e) how you feel about the treatment you receive and whether you are satisfied

(f) whether you will recommend the surgery to anyone else!

Thus, the way in which the telephone is answered vitally important.

Ring, ring

(Receptionist, picking up 'phone)	Dental Surgery.
(Potential patient)	Er, uhm, I haven't been before. Well I have, but not to you, ur, your dentist.
(Receptionist)	You want an appointment.
(Potential patient)	Yes, er well, yes.
(Receptionist)	Which dentist?
(Potential patient)	Um well, I don't know. My friend said, um, Mr, um, I can't remember his name.
(Receptionist)	Rodgers?
(Patient)	Yes, um, yes, I think that's it.
(Receptionist)	2.30 next Monday.
(Patient)	Oh, well, I don't ...Uur, yes, okay.
(Receptionist)	Name? That's 2.30 Monday 22nd. Thank you. Goodbye.

Try to imagine how you would feel. How could the patient's obvious anxiety and shortage of information be better dealt with?

Ring, ring

(Receptionist)	Good Morning. Mrs. Smith's practice. How can I help you?
(Patient)	Er, um, well I need an appointment.
(Receptionist)	Oh well, let's see now. Have we met you before?
(Patient)	Er no, I'm new to the area.
(Receptionist)	Oh, that's nice. Thank you for ringing this surgery. How did you hear about our practice?

(Patient)	Oh someone at work told me.
(Receptionist)	May I ask who it was?
(Patient)	Sandra Bloggs.
(Receptionist)	Oh you must work at the school. Mrs. Bloggs told you about us – she's great, we've known her for years. I think she's visiting us next week - would you like to come along on the same afternoon, then you will have no trouble finding us? etc., etc.

OR

(Patient)	I need an appointment. I got your number from the yellow pages.
(Receptionist)	Oh, so you haven't been here before?
(Patient)	No.
(Receptionist)	Are you having any problems at the moment?
(Patient)	No.
(Receptionist)	So, you'd like to register as a patient with us, and would like a check-up appointment?
(Patient)	Yes please.
(Receptionist)	Is there a particular day or time which suits you best?

The difference between the first and the second two conversations is that the latter are patient-centred. The receptionist is acting as a bridgehead between the dentist and the community. Receptionists are sometimes left in rather a dilemma. If the dentist appears to be 'the boss', the receptionist may naturally tend to be 'dentist-centred'. It is perhaps well to remember that a dentist without patients is not much of an employer and thus (even if for only cynical monetary reasons), the receptionist's concerns must lie primarily with the patient and not, as she might think, with the dentist. The receptionist is one of the practice's chief 'dental health marketing' tools; her personal manner and interpersonal skills may be vital to the success of the practice. Of the people who do not regularly attend the dentist, about half claim that the receptionist is instrumental in "putting them off".

The simple rules for anyone answering the telephone in general practice are that whoever answers the call should:

- Introduce themselves, both by name and by their role within the practice
- Enquire of the caller how they can help
- Refer to the patient by their surname, unless the patient asks to be addressed by their first name
- Attempt to establish how the practice can best serve that patient.

The dental team with the best communication skills in the world will not get the opportunity to utilise them if the first contact with patients, the telephone, is not used to its full advantage.

The experienced and organised receptionist will develop some type of system for remembering patients, their treatments and their circumstances. By doing so, the practice becomes more integrated into the community and therefore the first contact for new patients will become less and less of an ordeal.

Other barriers

Consider the circumstances of a student studying for an exam. He wants to do the necessary work and wants to pass the exam. However, actually sitting down and beginning the long hard slog is difficult to do. If his friends appear at the door and encourage him to go out, it will be hard to say no. Alternatively, the hapless student may convince himself that a trip to the launderette is vital, or that the dishes (hitherto unwashed for many weeks) must be done now. This example is given to illustrate that although we often have things which we really want to do, if any barriers to the task face us, it makes completing the task much more difficult.

A person may recognise their need for care and may consider a trip to the dentist to be worthwhile. The individual is not afraid although may be a little anxious. However, if faced with difficulties such as no transport to the surgery, or difficulty in parking, or lack of a route map, he or she will be less likely to attend. Such problems will also affect which surgery the patient is likely to go to.

Therefore, although organisational factors such as transport are not in themselves barriers to dental care, they may be used as rationalisations or excuses for non-attendance. They may also become 'costs' in the psychological sense, which might tip the balance in the patient's mind and make them favour a view that the 'costs' of a visit are not worth the benefits. Therefore, simple information about the best route, local buses, car parking plus adequate sign posting at the surgery will all make patients' visits easier, more likely to occur, more pleasant and less anxiety provoking.

The Receptionist

The role of the receptionist goes far beyond that which might be immediately apparent and obvious. As mentioned above, the receptionist is a crucial link between a community and a practice.

If you were a nervous new patient, walking into a strange, and to you, very threatening place, you are likely to feel more cared for, more recognised as a person, and more trusting, if you are greeted with "Hi, good morning, I don't think we've met you before", than by a busy, silent, white coat which is finishing some organisational task.

Nothing should ever be allowed to be more important than the patients' comfort and well-being. Waiting increases anxiety, as does uncertainty about the next step in the process. So, receptionists should **never** attend to practice business rather than deal with waiting patients (no matter how important the business seems and no matter how much the dentist is nagging for it to be completed!) and they should certainly not be discussing their holidays or the amazing habits of their loved ones while patients are waiting. Such behaviour immediately sends messages to patients that they are unimportant and powerless. If such messages **are** conveyed, it will be very difficult for the rest of the team to convince the patient that the practice and the team are there for the patient's benefit. First impressions set the tone for an entire dental visit and ultimately for the relationship between the patient and the practice.

The Dental Nurse

The dental nurse, in the first instance, and in the patient's eyes, forms the link between the surgery as a whole and the dentist and clinical work. Consequently the communication skills of the nurse are very important to the formation of a good relationship between the dentist and patient.

Simple courtesies such as the nurse meeting each patient in the waiting room and addressing them by name (title, e.g. Mrs. and surname unless invited by the patient to do otherwise) go a long way to ensuring patient satisfaction. The unseen voice of doom, echoing out from the surgery, through an open door or a tannoy, quite apart from making patients feel, once again, as if they are being processed through a system rather than cared for, is downright discourteous. Even in a full waiting room, the patient's case notes, combined with the nurse's memory, should be sufficient to enable identification of each individual patient.

The nurse needs to make the most of the short time she has to spend with the patient before clinical work commences, in order to form some sort of relationship with the patient. This is important, as the nurse must act as a support to the patient, as well as the dentist, during the patient's treatment. Compare the two following scenarios and decide which you would prefer to experience if you were the patient.

Scene 1   Dental nurse comes to door of dental surgery, calls 'Mrs. Smith' and returns inside surgery to autoclave the instruments from the last patient.

Scene 2   Dental nurse checks name and date of birth of patient, walks into the reception room, walks to the one female who appears to be about the right age, asks if she is indeed Mrs. Smith, introduces herself, asks if the patient is ready to see the dentist and takes her coat and umbrella to hang up. She then leads the patient to the surgery and performs an introduction.

The Clinician

Once the patient is inside the 'clinical' zone, their feelings of control over the situation are further diminished. It is therefore important that the clinician tries to involve the patient as much as possible in whatever process she is undertaking. Taking time to provide the patient with relevant information and allowing choices will enable the patient to regain a sense of control over the situation. This enhances patient satisfaction and dramatically reduces anxiety.

Although the dental team is familiar with the sights, sounds and smells of the surgery, it is important to remember just how terrifying a simple probe can look to a patient, let alone an array of instruments and important-looking equipment. If the dental team appear to be unconcerned about procedures that the patient (sometimes correctly) believes may be uncomfortable (and possibly painful), the patient's feelings of vulnerability will be enhanced. If, on the other hand, the team communicates that they recognise that items are causing concern, the patient's confidence will be enhanced.

Imagine a patient who enters the surgery, fairly relaxed and confident. They sit in the dental chair. As the hygienist chats away (believing he is making an excellent job of 'communicating' with the patient), suddenly, without warning, the chair is tipped back. The hygienist, noticing nothing untoward, continues to talk in a reassuring manner. The simple lack of explanation that the chair is about to be reclined:

- Increases the patient's sense of vulnerability
- Increases the patient's anxiety about what is to happen next
- Supports the patient's belief that the clinician does not understand their feelings
- Makes the patient think that no one will communicate the next step in the process.

The following chapters will develop the theme of how simple communication can substantially reduce a patient's anxiety. Chapter 4 details the moments in a dental visit that a patient may find most disconcerting and offers practical examples of how these sticky situations may be dealt with. However, in order that the dental team is able to detect problems and anxieties before they occur, the next chapter give some background information about the formation of interpersonal relationships.

Further reading

Batchelor P and Sheiham A. Does perceived risk of oral phobias influence the use of dental services in university entrants? *Community Dent Health* 2002 **19:** 116-119.

Gibson BJ, Drennan J, Hanna S, Freeman R. An exploratory qualitative study examining the social and psychological processes involved in regular dental attendance. *J Pub Health Dent* 2000 **60:** 5-11.

Newton JT, Thorogood N, Bhavnami V, Pitt J, Gibbons DE and Gelbier S. Barriers to the use of dental services by individuals from minority ethnic communities living in the UK. *Pri Dent Care* 2001 **8:** 157-161.

Pau AK, Croucher R and Marcenes W. Perceived inability to cope and care-seeking in patients with toothache: a qualitative study. *Br Dent J* 2000 **189:** 503-506.

Meeting Each Other

"This life's five windows of the soul
Distorts the Heavens from pole to pole
And leads you to believe a lie
When you see with, not thro', the eye"

William Blake

3

Introduction

Do you remember your first day at senior school? The first time you encountered the rest of your class? Did you not in some way classify or judge each and every person - even though you hadn't even spoken to many of them. There were the studious types, the hippies, the rebels, the "I'm going to be a prefect one-day" type. We all make immediate (and sometimes rash) judgements about people we meet.

We also find it disturbing when people leap out of the 'pigeon-hole' to which we've assigned them, and turn out to be completely different from how we'd imagined them to be. This stereotyping of individuals is a natural and necessary process that helps us to make sense of the world, but in the dental practice it can be somewhat unhelpful. If on first sight, you judge a patient to be a certain type of person (and which receptionist has not felt her heart sink as some people walk through the door?) we assign certain traits to them:

"Bound to be an appointment-breaker"

"Bet she gets stroppy about paying"

"Oh no, here's trouble"

and that judgement will taint the communication process thereafter. Also, in the same way that dogs can smell fear, patients will detect your expectations. Most people tend to live up, or down to the expectations which other people have of them. So, it's important to remember that a seemingly aggressive person might be as meek as a lamb, and an apparently quiet and nervous one may prove to be obstinate and difficult. The dental team are likely to attribute personality traits to each individual they meet, just as the patients are likely to make judgements about the members of the dental team. It is desperately important that everyone within a practice tries to keep the channels of communication as open as possible, particularly with patients who carry an aura of 'trouble' around them.

It is also true - largely thanks to the media - that the public stereotypes the dentist and the practice team. It sometimes feels as if admitting to being anything to do with dentistry is worse than declaring oneself to be a tax-collector or a traffic warden. Despite the best efforts of the dental professions, the dentist is still viewed as someone who doesn't mind inflicting pain on others - or worse, as someone who enjoys it. A recent children's radio programme featured two dentists, Mr. Black and Mr. Decker (Black 'n' Decker - get it!) who, (surprise, surprise) were the villains of the piece. Whilst such images continue to be portrayed, it will be an uphill struggle for dentists and their teams to convince people, particularly new and nervous patients, that they are health care professionals whose intentions are entirely honourable.

So how do we make judgements about people who we do not know?

We believe what we see - Non-verbal communication

A host of factors influence the type of person people judge us to be, and these are quite distinct from what is said between the parties concerned.

Dress and appearance

There is little doubt that people would regard a receptionist with cropped dyed hair, and a nose ring differently from one who had a more conventional haircut and did not adorn their olfactory organs with metal. Some people might prefer the former but, in general, patients expect their dental team to be relatively conformist, and to adhere to the 'status quo'. The important point is that we all make judgements about people based on what they are wearing, and what they look like. The clothes we wear signify a great deal. Members of a dental team, of course, often take this sort of communication to an extreme by opting to wear white coats. These are clearly not necessary for reasons of hygiene, but do convey important messages to patients about the dental staff's status as professionals, and the highly 'scientific' nature of the work. White coats and uniforms make us 'feel' different, both in ourselves, and to our patients. However, because emphasising the differences between the dental team and the patient, rather than the similarities, is unhelpful, perhaps ordinary, easily washed clothes might be more appropriate.

Facial expression

A very obvious clue to people's current state of mind (rather than their general personality type) is their facial expression. Facial expression is particularly interesting because the expression of one's emotions via the arrangement of one's facial features is an ability that is ubiquitous within the human race, and this form of communication can transcend cultural barriers. For example, basic emotions, such as sadness, happiness and anger are expressed facially in the same way in almost every part of the globe.

Have you ever been in a noisy place, where you cannot actually hear a word anyone says? If you observe the communication between people, they will laugh when others laugh, smile when others smile, drink when others drink - even though they haven't caught a single word of what is being said. Humans are very good at deciphering facial, not-so-coded, messages. Therefore, the dental team and the people who visit their surgery are constantly sending messages to each other by way of their facial expression, even if they don't realise it. We learn a great deal about how someone is reacting to what we are saying and doing, by watching their face. In fact their facial expressions will actually dictate to some extent, what we say and how we say it.

Eye contact

The oft (wrongly) quoted phrase about the "eye being the window of the soul" has a lot to recommend it. Eye contact and gaze is a crucially important part of non-verbal communication. Try the exercises below if you doubt this statement. You will need two people.

> Begin a normal conversation with each other whilst sitting in a mutually comfortable position.
> Continue the conversation.
> Person A shuts their eyes, whilst continuing to chat
> Person A opens eyes
> Person B stands, whilst continuing with the conversation
> Person B then walks to stand behind person A, whilst continuing the conversation
> STOP
> **Discuss with each other how you felt at each stage in the conversation.**

The length of time that two people in conversation spend looking at each other sends very important messages between them. Think of how much eye contact you have with:

- your dearest beloved
- a shop assistant
- a friend.

If you changed nothing in your relationships with these people, except for mixing up the lengths of eye contact, you will end up with some very confused people.

In general in conversation, people look at the other person for about 50% of the time BUT, mutual eye contact (where both parties look directly at each other at the same time) only occurs for about 25% of the conversation. We all know that increased eye contact is used as a particularly significant gesture. Mutual gaze is increased, even if only by seconds, between parties who find each other attractive. And most of us have felt disconcerted when the gaze of someone whom we find unattractive has rested upon us for just that split second too long. So, with patients, the ideal amount of eye contact is as in relaxed conversation. Gazing into their eyes will worry them!

The amount of eye contact a patient uses is also important for detecting non-stated worries. Negative emotions such as anxiety or depression will reduce eye contact.

Similarly the flow of the conversation is controlled to a large extent by the eye contact between the parties. A careful observer would notice that most patients tend to stop speaking, or at least slow their rate of speech when the clinician looks down to write notes. Thus, notes should be left to one side, particularly at a first meeting with a patient, or when trying to glean important information.

Posture

The posture of a person can give important clues as to their emotional state and their attitude to the other individual with whom they are conversing. If you were telling somebody something which you considered to be of great interest, if they were truly concerned with your story, would you expect them to lean backwards, or towards, you? Depending, to some extent on the position of the limbs, a backwards lean can suggest dominance, and if extreme, can be taken to be indicative of disinterest. In contrast, a slight forward lean, especially if combined with an open arm posture, indicates to the talker that you have interest and empathy with what they are saying. Any closed arm posture (i.e. arms folded across the body or crossed) can hint at rejection of what is being said. You will also notice that changes in posture often accompany a change of subject, or the end of a particular topic.

Like any other skill, practise is the key. Take the opportunity when socialising to observe the body language of people engaged in conversation. Try out various postures when you are talking and watch the reactions of the other person.

Proximity

As most of you will be aware, we all carry around with us a personal space - a sort of invisible 'bubble' which encloses each and every one of us. Human beings become stressed if someone else enters this portable 'territory', BUT, the size of the bubble, and what constitutes an 'invasion' depends on who the other person is, and what relationship they have to the individual concerned.

The first part of the zone is from zero, to about 18 inches away. The British are a notoriously non-tactile race, and in general they are only comfortable admitting lovers, very close friends and small children into this 'intimate' zone. In fact with the exception of children, 'touching' in public is almost completely limited to formal gestures such as handshakes, and that strange mutual jaw bashing gesture which women make when greeting each other (when they make kissing noises into the air next to the person they are saying hello to).

Think how uncomfortable you feel when other people enter your intimate zone uninvited, or worse, unexpectedly. Most of us have had the experience at parties, or other such social functions, of meeting people who insist on talking to you with their face only inches from your own. The most natural reaction is to step away. By making careful observation you can usually spot pairs of people pursuing each other round the room, invading and escaping, reinvading and re-escaping! These 'space-invaders' make most people highly uncomfortable - and yet think of the process of dental care. Dental professionals invade people's intimate personal space all the time. This invasion is sanctioned by the patient's relationship with the professional, but this does not mean that it is comfortable for the patient. It is therefore advisable to remember the stress that the simple act of coming so close to someone engenders.

The second layer of the personal bubble is from about 18 inches to approximately 4 feet. This is the characteristic distancing for interaction between people. Again, if complete strangers enter this layer of your bubble, you might feel disturbed. For example, most of us feel odd when squashed into a crowded lift, or on tube trains. (We tend to stare fixedly into the middle distance, avoiding eye contact). Similarly, when seated next to someone on a bus, train or plane for a long journey, it is usual for the individuals concerned to make some type of conversation - thus they become 'aquaintances' rather than complete strangers, and it becomes slightly easier to accommodate the other person within your territory. The same applies to dental patients. If they feel that they 'know' you, even only slightly, it will be less stressful for them to admit you into the space around them.

The next zone, from 4 to 12 feet, is the part of our territory in which we feel comfortable with others. In most offices, doctor's surgeries, and even shops the interacting individuals are separated by a distance of at least 4 feet.

Position

What is the optimal seating position if you are to engage someone in conversation? Again, it is useful to think of normal everyday social situations. People are usually only found sitting absolutely opposite each other in romantic restaurants or when engaged in combative discussion. Sitting opposite someone means that eye contact is inevitable and unavoidable. Therefore, the more comfortable and usual seating position for two people who are not particularly familiar with each other is at a diagonal angle. This enables eye contact to take place, but makes it avoidable when it might not be appropriate. It also suggests equality between the involved individuals. We cannot think of any situation in which one person voluntarily sits behind the other whilst chatting - except in the dental surgery. Such a position obviates eye contact and is most unnatural. So, conversation will be easier if you sit where a patient can see you. Repeatedly straining one's neck, trying to look at someone behind while you are talking, is most uncomfortable - and yet it is a position in which dental patients often find themselves.

Body contact

As mentioned above, touching other people is almost taboo, especially in the UK. It is the most basic form of non-verbal communication and requires invasion of the personal zone. Dental care requires that we not only touch the outside of a person's body, but continue the invasion into the oral cavity. We therefore completely violate a very strong social norm every time we examine or treat someone's mouth. And yet, often, we find it hard to understand why people are anxious about dental treatment despite evidence about the source of that anxiety being all around us in day-to-day life. Unfortunately, despite the publication of much research studying the importance of body contact between individuals, its impact on the dental patient is not a subject which has been fully addressed. We must therefore base our actions on what we know from our own experience of life and on observations of those around us. What is clear however, is that dental personnel often forget what is 'normal' for others, because of what is 'normal' behaviour for them. We must guard against this breaking of the usual rules of polite behaviour. Every action we make has consequences for the patient and affects how they feel about the process of dental care.

Do we say what we mean? - Verbal communication

Although we all know the general rules of conversation, knowledge of how best to go about a consultation with a patient can help to ensure that you gather accurate information quickly and efficiently, whilst maintaining rapport with the patient.

The open question

The 'open' question is one that allows almost maximum scope in the answer. Whilst it is a good idea to begin your conversation with a patient with open questions, you need to be aware that a question like: "How are you?" can elicit responses as varied as:

> "Fine" .... to those such as:

> "Well, I was at the doctor last week and he said to me that it wasn't right, you know, my chest. I mean he didn't actually say ...., etc., etc., etc."

The focused question

These types of question define the area of enquiry more closely than the open question, but still give the other person some freedom to add description and detail to their answer.

Q   "What sort of pain is it?"

A   "Well it's not too bad .... It comes and goes ...."

         OR

A   "Agony"

The closed question

These are questions that can only be answered by the response "Yes" or "No" or with a number, for example:

> "Do you brush your teeth every day?"
>
> "How many children do you have?"
>
> "What is your age?"

Such questions do not allow you to glean any extra information or detail.

So, if you begin a meeting with a patient with simple closed questions, you will miss important clues and cues about appropriate action. On the other hand, if solely open questions are used, the consultation may take an inordinate amount of time. It is therefore advisable to begin the conversation with more broad, open questions - ensuring during the patient's answer that all possible information from both the verbal response and non-verbal signs are noticed - then gradually narrow down towards more closed-type questions.

There are also questions that, although they will elicit a response, actually lead to false information being gathered.

The leading question

These questions imply a specific answer. Special efforts should be made to avoid these, because patients are often passive and will agree with the question's statement, even if it is not actually a true interpretation of the facts as the patient sees things. For example:

"You haven't been to the dentist for ages, have you?"

The compound question

Compound questions are those that ask for more than one piece or type of information. This sends a mixed message to the respondent and therefore you are bound to get a confused answer. A common example of such a question is:

"Do you brush and floss every day?"

If the patients answered "yes", do they mean they brush and floss every day, or do they brush once a week and floss once a day. Who knows?

Compound or double questions only serve to confuse everyone, so should be avoided.

Therefore, the types of questions that might be used are:

- Open
- Focused
- Closed

Those that should be avoided are:

- Double/Compound
- Leading

Obviously a consultation with someone is not, and should not be, a simple question and answer session. Various other forms of verbal communication will be used to put the patient at ease in order to enhance the rapport with which information is gathered and to ensure that the patient knows that you understand what he has said.

Social exchanges

Social exchanges are the polite, non-judgemental, greeting-type statements that are usually used at the beginning and end of a meeting in order to help to establish and maintain your rapport with the patient, for example:

"Good morning"

"Nice weather"

"Goodbye - have a nice day"

Facilitation

Facilitation is the term used for the general words and noises which we say and make in order to encourage people to keep talking, or expand on what they are saying, such as, "Uh huh", "Go on", "You were saying..."

Repetition

Repetition is exactly what it says, but is a very useful form of verbal communication. Again, this can readily be practised with very rewarding results at social gatherings. You simply repeat the last sentence, or part of a sentence which has been said to you. It will sound very obvious and forced to your own ears, but people find it very reassuring. It tells them that you are listening closely and are interested in what they are saying.

Restatement

Restatement is similar to repetition except that you take what is said to you and restate it in your own words, for example:

(Patient)   "I can't brush, 'cos my gums keep bleeding".
(Hygienist) "Mm, so you're having trouble brushing because of the bleeding".

Clarification/Interpretation

Again, this is similar to restatement in that you interpret a lengthy response into a statement of fact, and then check with the patient that your interpretation matches with what the patient feels.

(Patient)   "They only hurt when I eat, well drink, and even then it's not with everything. Tea, I can't drink tea, or coffee really".

(Therapist) "So your teeth only hurt when you drink something hot".

Reassurance, instruction, advice

These are self-explanatory. They usually occur towards the end of a dental visit.

A plea for plain english!

Much of this chapter has addressed the dental team's understanding and interpretation of what is said. A word or two is now required about the way in which dental teams express their views and findings to the patient. Just because a word is familiar and used every day among the members of the team, it is important to beware of the pitfall of assuming that it is equally meaningful to a patient.

Biological and medical terms, even ones that are used in everyday language can give rise to immense amounts of confusion. It is known that the terms 'anaemia' and 'heart disease' are often thought of as similar complaints by many members of the public. 'Palpitation' is also a word that can have a range of meanings to different people - to some it is a 'fright', to others it means a feeling of breathlessness. And the word 'flatulence' can, to some, mean an acid taste in the mouth.

So, care is needed in the way you express yourself, as you may not, to the ears of the listener, be saying what you think you are saying. Even a term such as gingivitis is completely meaningless to many people. Explaining to someone how to prevent something, when they have no idea what you are talking about, is very probably a gross waste of time!

The reasons why we slip **so** easily into 'jargon' are many. Firstly, complex biological terminology, including naming items in Latin, is sometimes used purposefully in front of a patient, in the mistaken belief that if they do not understand the language, it will reduce their anxiety about their problem. Secondly, use of a language that a second person does not know can be used to heighten the status of the first person. Doing so necessarily makes the second person feel powerless. Finally, jargon is sometimes used because there is an assumption that patients are 'ignorant', and will therefore be unable to understand medical ideas and biological/physiological systems.

Enhancing patients' sense of control over a situation is vital. The use of jargon only serves to do the opposite. It should be avoided - a dental team should feel that their professional status is compromised, not raised, if they need to resort to jargon. There is no shame in explaining things as they are. You would not like to be told about your medical condition in Cantonese, so why should dental patients not have the facts presented to them in an as accessible a way as possible?

Last thoughts

The whole purpose of developing your communication skills is that you are able to encourage people to disclose their problems and any other information you might need, in an efficient manner whilst letting the patient know that you care. In general, a successful meeting between a member of the dental team and patient is one in which the team spots associations between verbal and non-verbal signals, and picks up the points which are most important to the patient. Dental teams therefore need to develop their listening skills. Combined with appropriate postures and body language, those skills can go a long way towards encouraging trust and an atmosphere of partnership between patients and the dental team.

Further reading

Chambers S. Using non-verbal communications skills to improve nursing care. *Br J Nursing* 2003 **12:** 874-878.

Kacperek L. Non-verbal communication: the importance of listening. *Br J Nursing* 1997 **6:** 275-279.

Schouten B C, Hoogstraten J and Eijkman M A. Patient participation during dental consultations: the influence of patients' characteristics and dentists' behavior. *Community Dent Oral Epidemiol* 2003 **31:** 368-377.

Theaker E D, Kay E J and Gill S. Development and preliminary evaluation of an instrument designed to assess dental students' communication skills. *Br Dent J* 2000 **188:** 40-44.

What worries Patients about Dentistry?

"He had one particular weakness - he had faced death in many forms but he had never faced a dentist."

H G Wells
(Bealby)

4

Introduction

For the dental team, dentistry is a routine, relatively simple and 'normal' part of everyday life. It is vital, however, that they remember that the patient's view is very different. A dental visit for many is a rare occurrence, less than once a year for most people. People who visit dental practices are going to put themselves in a situation in which they will:

- Feel out of control
- Risk being reprimanded
- Have to lie down in front of someone (sometimes of the opposite sex - a very bizarre thing to do)
- Not know what is going on because they cannot see
- Be undergoing an operation while awake
- Potentially be uncomfortable, if not in pain
- Expose a sensitive and sensual part of their body
- Not be able to speak clearly
- Have to pay money for the privilege!

On reflection, it perhaps seems more odd that some people do voluntarily attend for treatment, rather than surprising that they don't!!

Below is a list of the potentially difficult moments in a dental visit that might cause anxiety, embarrassment, discomfort or worry for the patient. Anything that the dental team can do to help the patient through these situations will increase the patient's satisfaction and diminish their fear. Patients who are anxious and afraid are difficult and stressful for the dental team to deal with and to treat. Care at each of these points in the process of dental treatment will not, of course, ensure that every patient will be relaxed and happy, but the imaginative and empathetic team will find ways of dealing with these situations which will, at least, offer support to the patient when they most need it.

- Finding, and parking at, the surgery
- Appointment times
- Being on time
- Will I have to wait?
- How the practice is organised
- Being reprimanded
- Meeting the dentist
- The equipment
- The instruments
- The drill
- What will be done?
- Why is the treatment needed?
- Will it hurt at the time?
- Will it hurt afterwards?
- Will I be at work tomorrow?
- Lying down in front of unfamiliar people
- Having someone's fingers in your mouth
- Instruments in the mouth
- Being unable to speak clearly
- Having injections
- Having to spit in front of someone
- Will I be embarrassed by him/her?
- How long will it take?
- When do I pay?
- Who do I pay?
- How much will it be?

- Will they expose me to others as 'exempt'?
- Will I look odd afterwards?
- Will I be able to chew?
- Will they like me?

Getting there

Being unable to find where you wish to go is anxiety provoking for anyone, especially if there is a specific time at which your presence is expected. Therefore, as mentioned earlier, all new patients should be given instructions, preferably both verbal and written, as to how to find the practice, where the best (and second best) places to park are, **and** directions to the practice via public transport. Clear signposting of the practice will also help.

Being on time

Patients do not know how a dental practice is organised. They therefore do not know exactly when to arrive. If they are told that their appointment is at 3 p.m., should they arrive at 2.50 pm to 'check in', or will they have to wait anyway, even if they are on time? Also, many patients worry about the consequences of being unavoidably late (and yet you do not really want them to arrive early, as waiting will increase their anxiety). Will the receptionist tell them off if they are late, or the dentist? Will their appointment be given to someone else and will they have to pay for being late? All of these questions may arise in the patient's mind. Whether the patient is late or not, all of this uncertainty (especially if the patient is trapped in a traffic jam whilst worrying) increases their anxiety, which diminishes their ability to communicate. This in turn will result in a less than satisfactory relationship between them and members of the dental team. Patients, and particularly those who are new to the practice, should therefore be given precise details of what is expected of them in terms of time keeping and details of what they can expect from the dental practice.

How long will I have to wait?

Sitting in a dental waiting room (anticipating the treatment you might or might not receive, hearing the noise of the drill being used on others, watching other patients looking less than happy) for some patients, is the worst part of a trip to the dentist. Thus, the dental team must make all possible efforts to ensure that the practice is running to time. Obviously, delays are sometimes unavoidable. Simply saying that you are sorry about them having to wait, explaining why the hold-up has occurred and letting them know approximately how long they are likely to wait will at least allow the patient a choice as to whether or not they wish to stay, even if doing so does not reduce their anxiety and nervous tension.

How the practice is organised

When the patient arrives at the practice, what could be more disconcerting than a notice on a hatch (and we've actually seen this) saying 'Knock and Wait'. If nothing happens when the patient knocks, how long should they wait? If they knock again, will whoever is in there think that they are an impatient nuisance? If they don't knock again, and instead wait...and wait..., perhaps their first knock wasn't heard. What if someone comes out by chance, perhaps they'll think them stupid? How loudly should they knock?

We all feel silly when negotiating unknown systems and we all feel intimidated by situations in which we feel helpless and under the control of someone else. Therefore, patients need, if at all possible, to be given instructions as to how the practice is organised, **before** they get there. However, if this is not possible, the first entrance to the surgery should indicate to the patient how to proceed and what to expect, for example:

> Welcome to the Burnside Dental Practice.
> Please enter and turn left, where you will see the reception desk.
> The receptionist will assist you.

Being reprimanded

Almost every single patient worries about being 'told off'. Perhaps the receptionist will be cross if they are too early/too late, perhaps the nurse won't like it if they forget to leave their coat in the right place, the dentist will probably tell them that their mouth is unclean, and is bound to be displeased that their last visit was two years ago.

Research has shown that fear of reprimand is a very powerful barrier to dental attendance. It is therefore important that the dental team remember that, at the end of the day, the patient is a client, and can choose to go elsewhere. None of us are perfect and as the dental team we have no right to judge patients. If we do so and find them wanting, we certainly have no right to tell them so. Reprimanding patients, even if 'it's for their own good' will simply alienate them and is likely to make them less 'compliant' with our wishes, rather than more so.

Meeting the dentist

As stated earlier, the dentist has a powerful, stereotyped image to throw off before true communication can take place with a patient. Therefore, despite dentists' best efforts, patients are likely to find the dental surgeon an intimidating individual. Not only is the dentist someone who will have almost total control over them, she or he is also someone who carries a sort of 'professional mystique' and belongs to a 'high status' profession. The dentist may appear to be very clever, but may be judged as a very 'different' type of person by the patient, and such judgements will affect the relationship between the dentist and patient.

Anything the dentist can do to try to develop a sense of equality with the patient will be helpful. This might include ensuring normal social etiquette is observed, for example:

- introducing oneself
- discarding the white coat (which is worn more to indicate status than for any other reason)
- shaking hands on introduction
- engaging the patient in everyday conversation.

A particular point that might be raised here is the issue of names. It is increasingly common for people to use first names to address other people whom they do not know. Many people, particularly those of the older generations, find this odd, if not discourteous. Others find it acceptable. However, it is probably not appropriate to call a patient by their first name unless either you have been invited to do so or you have introduced yourself by your first name. For the patient to have to call you by your title, but to be referred to by their first name implies that you are more powerful and that the patient is subordinate. This is counterproductive to the ambience you wish to achieve.

The equipment

The equipment in a surgery is so familiar to the dental team that they probably almost do not notice it, let alone recognise its intimidating potential. It is however very unusual for people to walk into a room full of electronic gadgetry such as exists in a dental surgery. Thus, even though there may be insufficient time to explain the nature and use of every piece of equipment, the nurse, hygienist, therapist or dentist should, at the very least, recognise the fact that it may seem threatening to the patient.

"Does all this equipment bother you? I won't be using most of it."

"Try not to worry about all this equipment Mrs. Smith, we'll only be using the light and the chair today."

The instruments

As referred to earlier, it is hard to put oneself in a patient's shoes and realise that the all too familiar rack of excavators and root planers may look like instruments of torture to them. Again, explanation of their uses is the simplest and most effective solution, although rather time consuming. Alternatively, trays of instruments should be kept out of sight until they are being used. At that point, it is sensible to explain what the instrument is, and what it does, so that the patient still retains some control. Obviously the words used should be carefully chosen (for example, handpieces 'clean' decay out of a tooth rather than 'cut' it out).

The drill

The drill is the most commonly cited fear stimulus for patients. The noise seems to be particularly off-putting. Therefore, the drill should be run before using it in the mouth, in order that the patient may become accustomed to the noise. They should also be warned that you are about to do this! Similarly, it is necessary to remember that the noise of the drill when it is being used to cut a cavity sounds different to the patient than it does to the person who is wielding it, or to those nearby. It is helpful to express to the patient that you understand this, and know that it can be disconcerting. Many patients connect the noise of the drill with the experience of pain, and it is known that worries about discomfort might actually cause more problems than pain itself. Some patients are particularly worried by 'drilling'. In such cases, giving some control to the patient can be very comforting. Telling the patient that you will stop what you are doing if they raise a hand, or finger, increases their feeling of control. Many clinicians find that although the patient will often use the signal in order to reassure themselves that they do indeed have control, once they know that you will stop if they really want you to, they will find the procedure acceptable.

What will be done?

Much of patients' anxiety and feelings of lack of control stem from uncertainty about the treatment they will receive. Given that the procedures they may undergo range from an extraction (which is, after all, out-patient surgery) to simple advice and reassurance, this is understandable. This anxiety can be counteracted at a first visit by giving patients choices in their treatment. On subsequent visits, as long as the dialogue between the patient and practitioner is maintained, and all treatment plans fully explained, the patient's feeling of not knowing what to expect will be reduced.

Why is the dentist doing this?

Unfortunately, tales of patients undergoing unnecessary dental treatment abound in the media. Although repeated reports and a Government Enquiry have demonstrated that such unscrupulousness is extremely rare, patients have no way of knowing what is 'necessary' and what is not. Explaining your diagnoses to the patient and then **negotiating with them** (rather than telling them) what is to be done, will go a long way towards reassuring them that any treatment being undertaken is in their best interests. Patient satisfaction with treatment, and their acceptance of the costs, is greatly assisted by offering patients choices at the outset.

Will it hurt?

Pain, discomfort and dentistry are inextricably linked, at the very least in the patient's mind. However, when people are asked to explain what is 'worst' about a dental visit, the response "not knowing exactly what is going to happen" is more often mentioned than pain. Therefore, pain or discomfort seem to be tolerated, so long as they are explained, and the patient is warned.

"This might sting a bit."
"You'll feel a little pinch."

Clearly, as a patient's experience of dental treatment grows, and their relationship with the nurse and practitioner develops, they will come to worry less about pain being inflicted. No practitioner can promise a certainty of completely pain-free dentistry, and both experience and research findings suggest that it is not necessary to do so. If a patient understands what is to happen and why, their pain threshold can be remarkably heightened. The most important thing to remember is that anxiety and feelings of vulnerability lower pain thresholds. If a patient does experience pain, a supportive and empathetic dental team can do much to alleviate their reaction to it.

Will it hurt afterwards?

The dental team's entire day is spent dealing with oral disease. A patient usually only faces the practical clinical consequences of disease during a visit to a dental practice. Therefore, patients cannot be expected to know how long their anaesthetic will take to wear off, whether the pain will return, or whether the treatment will cause pain later in the day. The dental team must therefore give the patient as much information as possible regarding the natural history of their complaint/disease, and, as far as possible should advise the patient what action to take if certain circumstances arise.

"If it starts to ache when the anaesthetic wears off, take two paracetamol, then telephone if it is still painful tomorrow."

If this information is not given and explanations are not offered, untoward symptoms after treatment will engender distrust in the team, their competence and their honesty. Once again, knowing what to expect and knowing that the dental team can predict what will happen will make symptoms understandable and hence, bearable. Pain which one is not expecting is much more worrying than pain from a known cause.

Patients should also be advised as to how long their symptoms might last and whether or not they will be able to perform their usual daily activities.

Lying down

Would you find it natural to lie supine in front of someone you did not know? If you were intimidated by them or did not trust them, how comfortable would you feel lying down? Is it natural to rest your head between the knees of someone with whom you are not intimately connected? Of course not. And yet, although it breaks almost every social taboo in the book, dental teams expect patients to accept the adoption of the supine position as if it were something normal. Of course, to the dental team it is normal, but most certainly it is not a day-to-day occurrence for most ordinary people. Women especially find that lying supine in front of someone makes them feel very ill at ease. Whilst placing patients in this position is almost inescapable in modern dental practice, this does not mean that the patient will necessarily feel comfortable with it. There are three things that might help to alleviate this problem:

- Never tip the chair backwards without warning the patient, and asking their permission to do so

- Express to the patient that you recognise that to lie in front of someone is an abnormal, although, in the current circumstances, acceptable, thing to do

- Try not to leave the patient supine for any longer than is necessary, particularly when holding a conversation with them.

Fingers in the mouth

Would you not find it extremely disconcerting if someone with whom you were relatively unfamiliar put their fingers in your mouth? Similarly, would you feel comfortable if someone closely inspected a part of your body, which is both extremely sensitive and a sexual organ? And what emotions would you feel if suddenly your ability to communicate, both by talking and by facial expression, was suddenly rendered non-functional? This is exactly what we do to patients once we begin an oral examination. Although to do so is sanctioned by the professional status of the dental team, if you consider the questions above, it is not really surprising that dental treatment is considered to be, at its best, uncomfortable.

Unfortunately, there is little that can be done to avoid the discomfort engendered by a dental examination, except to remember that it is 'intimate'. The only suggestion offered here is that the team recognise that the patient is in a 'compromised' condition and that they avoid accentuating the patient's vulnerability. For example, some dentists attempt to diffuse the situation by somewhat ineffectually trying to make light-hearted conversation. The patient is of course unable to speak in response because of the instruments and fingers in their mouth and is unlikely to nod or shake their head for fear of moving some piece of equipment, currently positioned in their mouth.

Injections

Here, honesty is the best policy, although most patients prefer not to have needles waved in front of their eyes. The patient should always fully understand the purpose of the injection and have agreed that the procedure is necessary. Topical anaesthetic should always be used. Explanation of what is going to happen, and appropriate support for the patient as the injection takes place, usually makes the procedure acceptable to all but the most needle-phobic patients.

Spitting

It is almost unbelievable that the dental literature, even that which purports to describe, and lead to, understanding of the dentist-patient relationship, has never broached the subject of expectorating (spitting). To patients, spitting is spitting and they are being asked to spit in public. Spitting in front of someone is nowadays widely regarded as antisocial, rude, common and generally 'not done'. Most people find the thought of doing so in public absolutely mortifying. This is yet another social taboo which dental treatment ignores. The dental team, because they encounter expectoration every day, find it acceptable. For patients, to 'spit' is something **highly** embarrassing and this must be remembered. In particular, when a patient has undergone an inferior alveolar nerve block, the nurse needs to recognise that the patient will be embarrassed because they feel that they:

- cannot sip the proffered water properly
- cannot 'rinse round' without perhaps accidentally dribbling
- have little control over the 'spitting' process due to their numbness.

Most of us would be embarrassed to be seen by others with a long string of saliva dangling from our mouths!

It is moments like these that can make a dental visit quite excruciating for many patients, particularly the most personally fastidious. Sensitivity to both the patient's physical needs (a tissue) and their psychological embarrassment is required. Each patient will need to be handled differently, but of most importance is that the patient leaves the surgery feeling 'good' about themselves. Simply putting oneself in the patient's position is often a good start.

Will I be embarrassed by them?

Most patients brush their teeth vigorously before a visit to the dentist; even the most ardent smoker will forego a (much-needed!) cigarette for the dentist's sake; some will even avoid garlic in their evening meal the night before. All this is to avoid the dental team making less than positive judgements about them. If equality in the dental surgery is important for communication, do patients not deserve the same considerations?

We cannot count the number of times we have heard people say:

> "How come dentists always have bad breath?"
or   "I wish he'd sort his nose out before he treats me!"

These comments speak for themselves. Suffice it to say that it is important to remember the 'patient's eye view'. If everyone does so, embarrassment for all can be avoided.

How long will it take?

Most patients have other, more important demands on their time than dental treatment. If possible, when given an appointment time, a patient will need some sort of indication as to how long they should expect to spend at the surgery. No mother will make an appointment for 3.00 p.m. if she has to pick up her children from school at 3.30 p.m. But often, dental teams forget that the dental appointment is peripheral, rather than central, to the patient's life. It is usually, with dialogue, possible to arrange mutually acceptable appointment times and lengths. If this is done, it will avoid the half-completed treatment, or the patient who becomes increasingly agitated as the appointment goes on and on.

Again, it is desperately important to be honest with patients because if you are not, trust and confidence will be lost. The dentist should try to avoid saying 'nearly done' in order to gain compliance, when they actually expect to be whizzing away with the high-speed for another ten minutes. (Ten minutes to the team will seem like half an hour to a patient). In such a circumstance, especially if they are in a hurry, the patient will have two possible explanations, either you were lying, or, you didn't know what you were doing - neither of which conclusions will lead to good practice-patient relationship.

When do I pay?

Many patients worry, not about being unable to afford their treatment, but about discussing their treatment and its costs in front of others. Although many members of the general public will cite cost as a deterrent to having dental treatment, if questioned further, they have very little idea regarding how charges are set, who to pay or when to pay. This issue must be dealt with sensitively. Patients may feel that it is inappropriate to discuss money with the dentist in front of the dental nurse. Equally, many would prefer that the receptionist did not list their treatments and the attached costs in a crowded waiting room. Quite apart from the essential need for patient confidentially, information is once again the key to reducing the patient's anxiety. The procedure for paying and the costs of the planned treatment must be discussed at the outset in order to avoid embarrassment for the patient, and to allow informed choice.

A word here about the patient whose bill is paid by the State because they are unemployed or on a very low income. Many people still feel that there is great stigma attached to being unemployed and will avoid situations where they are made to feel 'different' or like 'charity cases'. Discretion regarding exemption from payment is always worthwhile.

How much will it be?

As stated above, many people, although they rationalise their dental non-attendance by citing costs as the deterrent, are actually totally uninformed about dental charges. People therefore fear the possible cost rather than make a reasoned choice that the treatment is not worth the cost. It is therefore essential to take time to explain how prices are set, and how much treatment will cost, before taking any action. If possible, choices and alternatives should be proffered.

Will they like me?

All of us like to feel that we are acceptable to other people. As should now be obvious, when unconsciously weighing up the worth of dental treatment, there are an enormous number of extra, intangible, and (to those in the profession) obscure hurdles to be overcome if a person is to decide to become a dental patient.

Last thoughts

Any efforts which dental teams can make towards giving their patients a psychological boost will be not only appreciated, but will act as a powerful practice marketing tool. It is easy to judge people and find them lacking. Each dental team member making a positive effort to find something good and endearing about every single patient will enhance the general ambience of the practice. It will also, incidentally and importantly, enhance the job satisfaction of the members of the dental team. Clearly, the key to patients enjoying (yes, enjoying!) their dental visits is for the dental team to make a constant effort to see things through the patients', rather than their own, eyes. Let's end this chapter with an observation - happy successful dental teams smile a lot. Whether this is a cause, or an effect, of their good relationships with their patients is open to speculation.

Further reading

Bergdahl M, Bergdahl J. Temperament and character personality dimensions in patients with dental anxiety. *European J Oral Sci* 2003 **111**: 93-98.

de Jongh A, Aartman IH, Brand N. Trauma-related phenomena in anxious dental patients. *Community Dent Oral Epidemiol* 2003 **31**: 52-58.

Kulich K R, Berggren U, Hallberg L R. A qualitative analysis of patient-centered dentistry in consultations with dental phobic patients. *J Health Communication* 2003 **8**:171-187.

Locker D. Psychosocial consequences of dental fear and anxiety. *Community Dent Oral Epidemiol* 2003 **31**: 144-151.

Motivation -
Yours, the Patient's and the Practice's

"You must be the change you wish to see in the world".

M.K. Ghandi

Introduction

If you were working on a tooth with a high-speed turbine that wouldn't cut because the engine was faulty, or you had difficulty when excavating a carious deciduous molar because the instrument was bent or corroded, would you continue trying to achieve your aim? Would you battle on regardless and end up with a 'botched-job' - or would you get fed up and change your instrument to one which worked properly?

No-one likes to work with unsatisfactory tools which don't function as they should. And yet, when we try to "motivate" patients and they do not respond to our exhortations, we tend not to address the real problem - our faulty tools or technique - but instead we blame the patient.

We have overheard a practitioner actually use the words: "my preventive chisel is blunt". He had recognised that, although he was trying his very best to run a preventively oriented practice, which was trying to encourage patients to behave in ways which would enhance their health, his progress was slow, unpredictable and was not getting worthwhile results. His frustration with his ineffective tools was evident, and just as he would give up with a faulty turbine, his demoralisation was affecting his commitment to prevention.

If we are to consider building a preventively orientated dental team that will benefit both the practice and the patients attending it, we need to have an appropriate and effective set of tools. If we are to encourage people to adopt behaviours which will enhance their health (and here it is worth reiterating that a patient's day to day behaviour will affect their health infinitely more than anything which is done within the practice walls) we need to know something about the mechanisms which affect what people do, why they do those things and how they feel about their actions. Perhaps the easiest way to seek such understanding is to examine ourselves.

Understanding our own and our patients' behaviour

Do you always, *always* do what you need to in order to achieve your personal goals? Do you smoke? Do you take sufficient exercise? Have you ever 'dieted' without losing a single pound? Do you ever drink more than the prescribed number of units of alcohol in a week?

Although doubtless there are some paragons reading this book, who are able to say that their behaviour is never counterproductive to their aims in life, most people will admit to the odd aberration! Consider again the students studying for exams. Although they are well aware of what needs to be done, often they will indulge in all sorts of distracting activities which they persuade themselves are necessary and essential. These other seemingly terrifically important occupations are at best inconsequential (tidying up the flat) and at worst counterproductive (going out and getting drunk). If you think hard about your own behaviours, you will recognise that you do not always follow the rational path that leads to the achievement of your goals.

And YET, as dental team members we repeatedly fall into the trap of thinking that if we merely inform our patients about what is helpful, or harmful (e.g. a healthy diet, brushing regularly, attending for all their appointments, taking all the tablets in the bottle) they will be good, sensible people and go and do these things. This is clearly a crazy expectation and flies in the face of the mountain of evidence which suggests that human behaviour is not based on rationality.

GOAL	ACTION
I will attend all the lectures I can	Misses two in a row because of being out late with new boy/girl friend
I will read the literature on a regular basis	Find brilliant novel which can't be put down Never reads dental journals
I will be nice to all the other staff AND all the patients	Has a bad day and bites receptionist's head off when a set of notes is unavailable
I will not drink too much	Goes to a party and drinks seven cans of strong lager
I will lose some weight	Passes cake shop with friend who is heavier still and both buy two cream cakes each

Since most of us know the consequences of our 'less than productive' behaviours, it is obvious that information, awareness and knowledge are quite insufficient as motivations to change the way we habitually behave. And yet we still tend to refer to the 'unmotivated' patient - and that patient, in turn, can demotivate the dental team who are committed to preventive behaviours.

The purpose of this chapter is to attempt to explain some of the processes that underlie behaviour and behaviour change in order that, if you wish to do so, you might use new ways to help to change your own and your patients' behaviours.

What stops you from wanting to change?

The first hurdle to be overcome when trying to change one's behaviour is overcoming the antipathy of one's friends and family when they tell you that the new way of life is silly. Imagine you wanted to take up hang-gliding. As well as the practical barriers - needing the time, appropriate place and circumstances, money, equipment and someone to tell you how it is done - if your nearest and dearest have an 'over my dead body you will' attitude, you are unlikely to achieve your goal of winging silently over the windy hills.

So, in order to take up a behaviour conducive to oral health, firstly a person needs to have:

- Enough time (can they spare an extra few minutes in the morning for brushing?)
- An appropriate environment (can you floss adequately when there is a queue of people knocking on the bathroom door?)
- The right material at their disposal (which toothbrush is best?)
- Been instructed in the necessary skills (why does it hurt when I floss when it's supposed to be good for me?)
- (Perhaps most importantly) People around them who also believe that the new behaviour is 'a good thing' (it's hard to avoid sweet foods if everyone laughs at you for doing so).

This may appear rather obvious, but it is necessary for dental teams to remember that it is a very middle-class assumption to believe that all of these requisites are in place. It is just not true that everyone has the time to take care of his or her personal health. For example, a mother's priority in the morning is likely to be getting the children to school, a teenager's priority may be an extra five minutes in bed. Furthermore, not everyone has a bathroom, let alone one that is warm and comfortable. If someone does not have an environment in which a new behaviour can easily take place, then it is quite simply unfair to suggest to them that their current behaviour is somehow unacceptable. Similarly, if a person cannot afford the requisites for oral hygiene, or dental treatment, imagine how they feel when told that these are things that they OUGHT to have. People are very unlikely to admit to such circumstances. Thus, before suggesting and/or expecting people to take up new habits for the sake of their oral health, the dental team need to know something about their patients' lifestyles and must treat the patients' circumstances with sensitivity and respect.

Finally, when someone wishes to take up a new habit or behaviour, if a physical action (e.g. brushing, flossing) is involved, with the best will in the world, the person cannot 'do' the new behaviour unless someone has shown them how to do it. For a physical skill, such as toothbrushing, a verbal description of the action will not suffice. If you are learning to play golf, your coach will stand behind you and physically manoeuvre your arms through the swing. By doing this repeatedly, you learn how it feels when the action is done correctly. With any physical activity, particularly those which require some degree of dexterity, it is always best to show the technique rather than explain it.

The process of change

Imagine again a person who has decided to make changes in their life. Giving up smoking is a good example to illustrate the steps towards change. Firstly, a person is unlikely to even consider giving up something that they enjoy if they are not aware that it is harmful. Most people know about the dangers of smoking - but this knowledge has come about via sustained information campaigns, powerful lobbying groups, dissemination of the results of trials, etc., etc. So, long before a person takes action, they gather information (sometimes almost subconsciously), then, once the thought that they ought perhaps to do something about their current way of life has arisen in their mind, they are sensitised to further information, and will listen carefully, and weigh up alternatives, and perhaps even ask for advice from people who have been through similar experiences. These two stages of behaviour change are called precontemplation and contemplation. If someone is at this stage, the giving of information is important to the continuation of the process but, receiving the information does not mean that the person will necessarily immediately change their behaviour. Precontemplation and contemplation are lengthy stages, and a host of other factors, which will be explained later, come to bear on the person, and will determine whether or not they take action as a result of the information gleaned.

It is vital that dental teams understand that these stages are an important part of behaviour change. This understanding will help the team to continue to give information even though they do not then witness immediate results from doing so. Information is necessary and is a prerequisite to choosing a healthy behaviour pattern and therefore dental health care professionals have a duty to impart it. However, understanding that giving information is only a part of the process is necessary if the 'preventive chisel' is not going to be thought of as useless and blunt.

The next two stages of behaviour change are action and maintenance of action. Again, it is vital to recognise that these are not ends in themselves but are part of a process. The next sections will attempt to describe how and why these stages may be temporary, and what the dental team might do to help actions to become habits.

A further part of the process of changing behaviour is relapse. Relapse occurs when a person returns to their old habits. This is almost inevitable, and it is important to expect it, and support rather than reprimand people in this stage. If a patient is made to feel like a naughty child when they fail to maintain a new behaviour, they will be alienated and are likely to return to precontemplation. Support and reassurance that their slip-up is not the end of the world is vital if they are to return to action. Let us go back to the smoking example. The new 'non-smoker' has not touched a cigarette for two months. All the friends and family have stopped saying: "O clever you, stopping smoking, you're doing really well" and have assumed that the reformed smoker is now a non-smoker. At a party, with inhibitions and strength of mind at a low ebb, the reformed smoker thinks: "I'll just have one, a few puffs won't hurt, I'll be off them again tomorrow", and proceeds to take a proffered cigarette. The next day, if the person's family and friends take the attitude that the smoking person is a failure, and make it clear that they consider the person to again be a smoker, that is exactly what will happen, the individual will return to being a smoker. If however, supportive peers remind the person that they are a reformed smoker, that parties don't happen every day, that the cigarette was an understandable slip and that they can now resume their non-smoking persona, the smoking habit is much less likely to begin again. Therefore, continued support for a new behaviour is required for a long time, particularly when the individual concerned is finding things difficult.

Remember, making people who have tried something new feel like a failure when they do not immediately succeed is highly counterproductive. It is sometimes referred to as 'victim-blaming' because the person who is suffering is also receiving the blame for their state. It only serves to make the person wonder why they wanted to change in the first place -since doing so only seems to get them into 'trouble'!

Keeping the new behaviour going

Very few of us will do anything unless there is something that we truly want which can be achieved as a result of our actions. This section deals with how we learn about the consequences of our own actions.

Conditioning

Classical conditioning

Let us begin with Pavlov and his poor unfortunate dogs. As you will know,

Pavlov noticed that his dogs salivated when they were fed. He then consistently rang a bell at the dogs' mealtimes, and, after some time, could demonstrate that salivation could be stimulated by the ringing of the bell alone, even in the absence of food.

What Pavlov had demonstrated was that autonomic reflexes (bodily functions which occur naturally as a result of certain stimuli) can be conditioned to occur by repeatedly pairing the conditioning stimulus (the bell) with the unconditioned stimulus (the food). Of what consequence is this to a dental team you might ask? Well, consider the person who only attends a dental practice when they are in pain. They then (because radical treatment is often required for end-stage disease) undergo unpleasant, uncomfortable and sometimes painful treatment. Dental visiting is therefore paired with discomfort and pain. Discomfort and pain quite naturally cause avoidance behaviour. They also, quite naturally, cause fear, anxiety and the physiological signs which accompany such feelings: sweating, shaking, pallor, etc. Thus the patient is conditioned to react to dental visiting in a way which simulates the reaction of someone threatened with a painful experience.

Operant conditioning

Of much greater importance in relation to behaviour is operant conditioning. The theory of operant conditioning is that the consequences of any action determine the likelihood of that action occurring on a subsequent occasion. Put simply, if something nice happens after you have taken a particular action, you are more likely to take the action again. If something unpleasant happens as a result of your action, you are less likely to do it again.

For example, consider toothbrushing. The action of brushing may elicit a reward or positive reinforcer, because it makes the person's mouth taste and feel good. However, if gingivitis is present and the mouth bleeds and feels uncomfortable after brushing, the consequences of the action are unpleasant. In the first instance, brushing is more likely to happen on a subsequent occasion and in the second example it is less likely.

The importance of the consequences of an action can be enhanced by other people. Thus, praise and encouragement for an action act as powerful reinforcers. However, it is essential to remember that things which the dental team might consider to be 'rewards' (such as reduction in caries rates, healthy mouths, enhanced chances of retaining teeth) are not necessarily powerful rewards to someone else. Thus, if the principles of operant conditioning are to be used to encourage behaviour change, it is important that the dental team discover from the patient what factors are personally relevant. For example, stressing to a teenager how much more kissable they might be with a clean mouth is much more likely to encourage oral hygiene than the prospect of them having a healthy dentition and gums in ten years' time.

The power of consequences to act as a reward are directly related to how closely in time they occur after the action. For example, imagine a patient who is trying to reduce their consumption of sweet foods and drinks in order to prevent dental disease. They are then offered a toffee bar. The rewards from eating the toffee are sweet taste and satisfied hunger, both of which are very immediate consequences. The reward from not eating the toffee is health in the future. Even if for the person concerned, the health consequences are MUCH more important than the taste and enjoyment of the snack, psychologically the immediate rewards will be more enticing. Although the health rewards of a behaviour are more important, the time needed to achieve that reward means that the incentive is less 'weighty' than the immediately available (although less valuable) consequences of the behaviour.

Knowing about operant conditioning gives the dental team important clues about specifying rewards that will determine behaviours. Always stress the immediate rewards which a patient will experience from a desired behaviour, rather than the long term ones, e.g. kissability in a teenager, feelings of self control when a snack is rejected, short-term improvements in appearance.

Cognitive dissonance

However, when deciding whether or not to take up a health related behaviour, a process called dissonance is also relevant. Dissonance occurs when someone believes that one 'action' is best but does something else. For example, a mother who believes your recommendation that her child should eat fewer sweets will feel some sort of psychological discomfort when she gives some of the 'forbidden' foods to her offspring. She feels dissonant. In order to relieve her dissonant position, she can do one of two things.

Firstly, she may alter her belief in some way:

> "I know sweets cause decay but I'm sure I don't give enough for it to matter."

"I'm sure that hygienist can't be right – she's just keeping herself busy telling me these things."

"I know I shouldn't give Kylie these, but she's got very strong teeth - it might affect others but it won't matter with her."

"I'll make sure she brushes her teeth extra well tonight, then it'll be okay."

or, she may alter her behaviour:

"No more sweets from now."
"I'll give her less than I used to."

Whether it is the belief or the behaviour that changes will depend on the amount of positive reinforcement for each. So, it is easy to see that the beliefs might be altered by the attitudes and behaviours of others. If all the other mothers at the school gate give their children sweet foods and drinks, it will be easy for the mum to believe that her behaviour is better than others and therefore cannot be damaging.

Alternatively, if social support and praise are available for the behaviour change then it is more likely to occur. Here, it might be worthwhile to remember that silencing a screaming tot is a very powerful reward for sweet-buying to a harassed mother.

Consequences of, and antecedents to, behaviour

So every piece of behaviour that we undertake has a consequence. How likely a piece of behaviour is to recur will depend on whether this consequence acts as a reward. However, as should be evident from the above examples, the circumstances which precede a behaviour pattern are also important (as above in the example of the party at which a cigarette is offered to a reformed smoker, the toffee being offered to someone who is making efforts to reform their dietary pattern, the circumstances in which a mother finds herself when faced with denying her child sweet foods). These circumstances are called the antecedents to behaviours. For example, you will take a biscuit from a plate offered to you, even though you neither want one nor like them. Therefore, it is important to remember that although patients may wish to change their behaviours for the sake of their health, the environment in which each decision takes place will have an important bearing on what actions occur.

This can be useful. If a person showers and shaves every single morning but their oral hygiene practices are intermittent, encouraging them to make the likely behaviours (showering, shaving) dependent upon the unlikely behaviour (toothbrushing) can be helpful. By training themselves to do this, the person is rearranging the antecedents and consequences of a desired behaviour, and it is more likely to become a habit. So, with each person, try to find some habitual behaviour with which the new, desired behaviour can be paired.

Considerations for behaviour change

Knowledge
Conditioning
Dissonance
Antecedents and Consequences

Self efficacy and locus of control

People may regard doing something new as: something they want; something they know how to do; and as something which they think will bring a reward and yet still they are unable to take up the new behaviour in a committed, long term way. Why is this?

You will at some time have contemplated changing your life in some way. You have found something you want to do, and know how to do, but you don't do it.

Taking more exercise is a common resolution which people make yet many find their new regimes difficult to begin or difficult to adhere to. The point is that if you want to become fitter but are not confident that you will go for your run every day (because it's obviously not worthwhile to only run once or twice) then you are unlikely to even start to try to do so. The belief in oneself, belief that one can do something when one puts one's mind to it, is called self-efficacy. If people truly believe that they just can't manage a new behaviour pattern, they won't bother trying. For this type of person (or yourself) it is important to identify something in the past where they have achieved something through being determined. This might be passing an exam, taking a driving test, or achieving the 30 metres breast stroke swimming badge. Anything at all can be used to point out to people that their belief that they can't stick to something and achieve their goal isn't true. Other means can be used to enhance this confidence in one's ability to "get there". Simply hearing people say that they believe that the person can achieve the goal will go some way towards enhancing the sense of self-efficacy. Seeing someone similar achieving success can also be helpful.

Unfortunately, there are also people who have an attitude, when faced with a challenge, of, "Yeah, 'course I could do that - but what's the point? I couldn't be bothered". These individuals have a strong sense of self-efficacy and are confident about their ability to change themselves. However, they will not go to the trouble of doing so because they are not convinced that the effort made will bring about improvements in their life. The decision not to change is based on the person's estimate of how likely the desired outcome is. People who feel that ultimately the way their life turns out is dictated by others (or luck, or fate, or a higher being) have what is called a low internal locus of control. They believe that the results of their behaviours are not in their own hands but are controlled elsewhere. The dental team can help such patients, firstly by setting small, easily achievable goals (outcomes) and by offering great praise and encouragement for any improvement, no matter how small. This will serve to point out to the person that what happens, at least to their mouth, is largely a consequence of their own actions. This can become hugely important for people who have a low locus of control. At last they may find something that they themselves can influence.

This sense of control over outcomes is very important. As has been mentioned earlier, a person's personal hygiene and diet-related habits have the most profound influence on their oral health. It is therefore essential that patients understand that control over their health is largely in their own hands. It is desperately important that the dental team encourages people to consider their teeth to be their own responsibility and not that of dental professionals. However, certain dental practices are run in a way that makes people feel powerless (see Chapters 2 and 3). Thus, a trip to the dentist can markedly reduce a person's internal locus of control. By running a dentist-centred practice, the dental team send very powerful negative messages to patients about the extent of their own role in their own oral care, i.e. the dental practice takes responsibility for the patient's mouth, and the patient is not 'allowed' to be involved. This is the exact opposite of what we wish to achieve. We do not want to encourage helplessness and dependence in our patients. Therefore, if we truly wish to run practices that operate for the benefit of patients' oral health, we must ensure that the ambience of a dental visit is one of being patient-centred and patient controlled.

We often send very mixed messages to patients about who is 'in control'. Generally, we take all the responsibility away from a patient and act as if they are passive accepters of care whilst they are in the surgery, only to send them away telling them to take actions to care for themselves. Oral health is enhanced if the patient is consistently treated as the person who is 'in the driving seat' as far as their oral health is concerned and much can be done in the surgery to ensure that this occurs.

Setting goals

Throughout the process of behaviour change, it is very important that the involved parties are very clear about that which they are trying to achieve. Not setting clear goals is certain to lead to failure. Statements such as:

> "You need to improve your oral hygiene."

do not make it clear to the person what it is they need to do, or why they might want to do it.

In contrast:

> "You'll find your breath is much fresher if you can clean around the back of your last tooth - I'll show you the plaque there today and we'll try to half the amount by your next visit. The way to reach it is ...."

The second statement:

- Gives the patient a personally relevant reason for taking action
- Makes it clear what is to be achieved
- Offers them a technique whereby the goal can be achieved.

Making precise statements regarding why the patient (rather than the dental team) might want the behaviour to change, offering an exact and achievable goal and remembering to demonstrate the appropriate techniques, is vital.

Last thoughts

Patients are individuals. It is not possible to describe a means by which all patients can successfully become orally healthy. This chapter is included in order that the dental team can offer support and help patients if they want to change. It should be clear from what has been said that if there is one key to helping patients to satisfaction with their oral health, it is communication. Without good communication skills, the dental team can neither decide what information a patient wants or needs, nor identify the stage of change which the patient is at. They will also be unable to glean the necessary information about the patient's current beliefs and behaviours. Without a high degree of interpersonal skill, dentists and their teams cannot possibly identify rewards and incentives that are appropriate for each individual patient, nor will they have sufficient insight into the patient's lifestyle to allow an understanding of the barriers to, and antecedents and consequences of, behaviours that are relevant to the individual concerned. A good relationship with patients will help the team to utilise and enhance patients' beliefs in themselves and support the patient's sense of control and responsibility for their own health. Most importantly, it will allow them to communicate the necessary incentives, goals and skills in an effective way. The external influences on our own and our patients' behaviour are myriad. Suffice it to say, once again, that oral health is only a tiny part of most people's lives. However, being socially acceptable and fitting well into one's peer group is desperately important to almost everyone. These more innate needs do have a connection with oral health. It is up to the dental team to recognise how their own goal (oral health) fits with these more profound influences.

Important influences on behaviour:

- Friends, peers, family social group
- Improvements to life, positive consequences
- Negative consequences, especially of difficult behaviours
- Good outcomes in relation to the effort
- Environment (social and political), lifestyle
- Realistic goals which can definitely be achieved.

Further reading

Armitage CJ, Conner M. Efficacy of the Theory of Planned Behaviour: a meta-analytic review. *Br J Soc Psychol* 2001 **40:** 471-499.

Draycott S, Dabb A. Cognitive dissonance. An overview of the literature and its integration into theory and practice in clinical psychology. *Br J Clin Psychol* 1998 **37:** 341-353.

Elder JP, Ayala GX, Harris S. Theories and intervention approaches to health behavior in primary care. *Am J Prev Med* 1999 **17:** 275-284.

Reisine S, Litt M. Social and psychological theories and their use for dental practice. *Int Dent J* 1993 **43:** 279-287.

Neuro-Linguistic Programming

6

"Listen, or thy tongue will keep thee deaf"   American Indian Proverb

Introduction

Chapter 3 detailed the basic foundations of good communication. This chapter very briefly introduces a further theory of communication between individuals – Neuro-Linguistic Programming (NLP). It is important to recognise that the next few pages give only the merest glimpse of NLP. Huge amounts have been written on the subject and this short chapter cannot possibly do anything, other than introduce the topic. Therefore, if this chapter interests you, it would be best to read further from some of the many books on NLP which are available.

The magic of NLP

Twin girls, with fairly elderly parents, went to see their local dentist about five and a half years ago. When the nurse met them in the waiting room, they were sitting like Tweedledee and Tweedledum, with their arms folded, and were, the nurse thought, going to be 'difficult'. They were nasty, recalcitrant teenagers (we've all been through that stage!). After much persuasion, much shouting from their mother and threats from their father, they got as far as the surgeries. They each went in, each refused to sit on the treatment chair and each sat sullenly, eyes cast down, not speaking. The nurse left two hygienists to do what they could. After half an hour, Elizabeth and Ruth came out of the surgeries. Elizabeth was bubbling with self-importance, telling her mother what she needed for her teeth (new toothbrush, sugar-free drinks, a filling at the next visit) and was describing the treatment she had had. Ruth was still looking down, had not been examined and simply looked the other way when another appointment was suggested.

So, what was the secret of Elizabeth's turn around? What had that hygienist said or done to convince Elizabeth that healthy teeth were what she wanted? What was it about the way the hygienist had reacted which had got Elizabeth 'on side'? This chapter describes a concept that might explain Elizabeth's hygienist's success and Ruth's hygienist's failure to 'get through' to the patient concerned.

NLP is a field of psychology that examines the way different people think and communicate with each other. The theory was developed by observing therapists who were successful with their clients. It was observed that, although all the therapists worked differently with their patients, there was one thing that the successful ones had in common. They were very good at gaining their clients' trust. In this chapter, we attempt to show how gaining patients' trust is: necessary if you are to successfully 'sell' oral health, vital if you are to work in a successful practice, and essential if the dental team are to feel happy and unstressed.

So, what was it about Elizabeth's hygienist, which made her 'brilliant' at getting what she wanted from the patient? And why is it that, even for people who are 'brilliant' with patients, they find some people easy to deal with and others difficult? That is a bit like asking why do some people like one person and not like another? Well, NLP suggests that it is trust which makes the difference. Trust is what makes us successful (or unsuccessful) with patients. If a patient trusts you, they will attend for their appointment, undertake care of their teeth when you are not there AND will accept treatment (even complex, difficult, uncomfortable treatment) with equanimity.

What NLP does is explain why trust develops in some, perhaps most, of our relationships with patients, but sometimes it does not.

Perceiving the world

We all have different ideas about reality - you have a slightly different way of perceiving the world from me, or the person you live with. But we automatically trust people who look at the world in a similar way to ourselves. When you feel understood you give people your trust. If you think someone understands you, you open up to them more easily.

If you master the techniques described in this chapter you will:

- Know more about a person in five minutes than you previously could in two weeks

- Learn to predict what your patients want and what they will do

- Learn how to get your patients to want to make themselves healthy.

So what is trust, how is it formed between you and your patient? Why do some teams get patients to trust them so thoroughly? Below are some tips to help you understand how and why trust is built between people.

Neurolinguistic programming

We all have three basic methods of perceiving and interpreting the world around us.

Exercise 1

Find a partner to do this exercise with. Label each person A or B. For two minutes, have A describe to B their first half hour of wakefulness this morning. B listen carefully, testing your ability to understand your partner.

We will return to this exercise later.

NLP suggests that each person can communicate visually, auditorially or kinaesthetically.

If you are a visual person, you see the world. If you are auditory, you hear the world and kinaesthetic people feel the world. Of course, each of us can see, hear, and feel, but if you think of all the stimuli your brain is receiving at any given moment - the words written on the page, the feel of your chair, etc, etc., you will realise that we need a way of organising all that information. And each of us organises it according to our own mental map, then, having done so, we decide how to respond.

Now all behavioural theories make things tidier than they really are. So, for example, in the same way that no one exclusively has socks in their sock drawer – no one thinks exclusively in visual or auditory or kinaesthetic mode. We switch back and forth BUT, almost everyone has a preferred way of thinking; everyone is more comfortable with one rather than the other: we all feel one or other of these is the most natural way of understanding the world.

Your preferred mode of communication is the one you use when you are most relaxed or unguarded. Your preferred mode is also the one to which, if someone communicates to you using it, you give the strongest reaction.

Visuals

We know a dental student called Catherine North. She can cut a crown prep in seconds and she is generally regarded as a phenomenon. We asked her about her talent and she said this: "I just see it. I draw the shape in my mind. I focus on the burr going into the tooth at just the right spot and see what I'm going to do. Then I just do it. It's all clear in my mind at the start."

Notice the word Catherine used so often in that response. She sees it. She sees what she's going to do. And she draws it, focuses on something, it's all clear to her. She understands what to do because she sees things. She makes images, which guide her through the whole process. If she couldn't visualise her finished preps, she couldn't do them so well.

And about 35% of the people who read this book will be visuals. That 35% understand things better if they see them. Visuals' minds turn everything said or read into pictures. If you discuss something with them in visual terms they smile. If you describe things pictorially, visuals comprehend - and they become VERY comfortable with you.

When you talk to a visual, they run a sort of video film in their head. They understand your words by comparing them to the associated pictures. They are looking at images the entire time you are speaking. Visuals are great witnesses, they can describe things in minute detail - colours, shapes.

So, how can you tell when a person is thinking visually? The words and phrases they use give one clue. Another factor about visuals is that what you look like is very important.

I once did a talk that seemed to be well appreciated. Afterwards I was talking to people and a woman came over and said: "I enjoyed that very much, but I missed a lot of the beginning – you had a bit of hair sticking up." (And then she fixed it). "I couldn't concentrate for ages", she said. (Most irritating for me, as I had been trying so hard to communicate)! The point is, there are people who are bothered by asymmetry in how you look or perhaps in how your surgery looks. So, dressing correctly for patients (white coats for instance, may be appropriate even though they seem unnecessarily formal) may be very important. Many patients will be distracted if something about you is 'off' visually. If you don't look good, getting visuals to trust you will be harder.

Eye movements

Now, we get to the nitty gritty, and we believe that eye movements give the most important clues to people's mental maps. If you take videotape recordings of people interacting with each other, and study them really carefully, you'll find a link between the way people think, and the way they move their eyes. Watching people's eye movements as you listen to what they're saying will give you a very strong indication of how they are thinking *(Figure 6.1)*.

Ask someone about their future – for example, where they see themselves in five or ten years' time and watch what their eyes do. Then ask them about something in the past – a house they used to live in perhaps. Again, watch their eyes.

Visuals, when creating images, when thinking about the future look up and to the right, and when thinking about the past move their eyes up and to the left.

The third thing they may do is gaze ahead for a few seconds, eyes slightly out of focus. That glazed expression doesn't mean a visual person isn't interested in what's going on - she's synthesising thoughts, letting images sink in.

So practise with a friend, it takes about a week to start to really read eye movements but it is a really powerful tool. Imagine you have a patient who needs a lot of treatment and is just on the brink of committing themselves to a self-care regime.

Patient: "I really want to keep my teeth, but Mr. So & So said they were
            okay - he didn't mention all this flossing, etc."
Hygienist: "What did he say?"

Patient: "He said they'd be fine."

If the patient's eyes go up and to the right she's lying! She's constructing an image of a dentist saying and doing things that haven't actually happened. If the dentist really said those things, and she's remembering, then her eyes will look up and to the left. That gives you an enormous clue on how best to proceed.

Eye movements won't tell you everything, but they will confirm your hunches. If you constantly check and recheck your patients' eyes when they talk, you will get a great deal of information.

Auditories

The next group to consider are slightly rarer. These are the auditory people.

Jimmy Connors the tennis player is an auditory. You maybe remember that he was a brilliant tennis player - particularly his return of serve. Someone once asked him how anyone could hit a ball which was coming towards him at nearly 140 mph and he said something like this: "I listen to how the ball sounds as it comes off the server's racket. I can hear if it's got top spin, if it's been sliced. I can hear what the ball's gonna do". He listens and can decide what to do, where to be on the court from interpreting sounds. Quite amazing. Auditory people listen to the way you say things. They listen more to how you say it than to what you say. So your voice, its pitch, timbre, the intonation, transmits more to a person with an auditory mind map than anything else.

Think of an auditory person as having a mind like a juke box, one of those old 1950s ones where the arm actually went over and grabbed a record, put it on the turntable, the stylus came down and then the record played. When an auditory person hears something he reaches for a 'record' – then, once he knows what song you're singing, he understands.

Auditories love the telephone, they respond to sounds more than anything and they say things out loud that they don't mean. People who mumble or talk to themselves are usually auditory.

Auditories tend to speak rhythmically and they breathe slower and deeper than people with visual mind maps and some psychology researchers believe that you can recognise when a person is thinking auditorially because they'll touch their faces when they're listening. So the next time you have a patient who talks to you with a hand up to his or her face, look at their eyes and listen for 'sound' words, like 'say', 'tell', 'hear'.

When people think in an auditory way (and this will usually happen if they are thinking about a conversation), they have different eye movements from visuals. If their eyes go directly to the right, they are probably thinking about a future conversation. For example, "I wonder if my boyfriend will laugh if I say I have to have a brace?" "I wonder what my dad will say about me needing to come here every week?"

If on the other hand a person in auditory mode looks left they are thinking about the past. So, ask the questions you need information about, then watch their eyes.

"Tell me, what advice did the hygienist give you?"
"Could you tell me who said that your teeth need bleaching?"

When people try to recollect something like a conversation they are in auditory mode and will look side left.

One other eye movement is common in auditories - they look down and to the left. That means they are trying to make sense of what you are saying. They are in effect talking to themselves, running tapes in their heads, comparing what you're saying to what they've heard before. So, when your patient looks down and left, STOP. Stop talking, let his internal conversation play itself out. If you keep talking, he won't hear you.

Kinaesthetics

So, 25% of us have auditory as our preferred mode of communication and 35% have visual as their preferred mode - what about the other 40%?

Think back to Excercise 1 (page 62) and try to remember if you talked about 'feelings', 'hunches', 'emotions'. If you did you were probably in kinaesthetic mode.

People who talk about feelings are kinaesthetics and kinaesthetics get their information from touch and from emotions. Funnily enough, people whose preferred mode of communication is kinaesthetic often get goose bumps. They're impulse buyers, they just like or dislike people. They only trust you if they get a good feeling about you.

Some people are always keen to hear about others' home lives, or their emotions - those people are kinaesthetics. They want to access feelings. Kinaesthetics are touchers. Some people touch others a lot and others do not. And some people are always fiddling with pens, paper clips, erasers. They play with things. They also tend to be sensitive to temperature and often feel too hot or too cold. The important thing to recognise is that when a kinaesthetic is physically uncomfortable, it will be very difficult for them to concentrate on anything else and it will be very difficult for them to listen to you. So, when a patient is lying on the dental chair, with a matrix band poking out of their mouth, if they are kinaesthetic, any information you convey to them will be wasted.

Kinaesthetics also pause a lot. If you say: "Do you think you'll manage the flossing?", the typical kinaesthetic will say:

"Well, I think that .... mmmm ..... I understand ...... mmm ....how to do it ..... I've got the hang on ...."
The reason for the pauses is that the person is trying to get a feeling, "How do I feel about flossing?". They will talk when they've got a feeling. Don't dismiss them as dumb/stupid because they talk slowly.

When people are checking out their emotions about something, they will look down and right. So, if your patient is looking down and to the right they are accessing their feelings. Give them time to respond. You haven't lost them, they're just trying to understand what they feel about a particular situation.

The importance of NLP for the dental team

You have to be aware of your preferred mode of communication to avoid conversations in which you think you are saying one thing and the patient is understanding the information completely differently from the way you intended.

If you're very strong in one mode, you might find it difficult to remember anything in other modes. Some people can remember conversations almost word for word. If they have been told something they don't forget it and can repeat it exactly BUT those same people would make the most appalling witnesses. People who can never remember anything about who was at a scene, or what colour or make of car they have seen, are strongly non-visual. People who remember names but never know whose face they belong to are not thinking visually. People who cannot describe what they pass on a route they drive every day are probably auditory or kinaesthetic. In contrast, people who are good at remembering faces and who are good spellers are probably visual.

The kind of person who massages shoulders, or hugs people a lot, the sort who touches, slaps backs is probably kinaesthetic.

So, why should you want to know which you are, and why is it important for oral care personnel to recognise and read other people's natures? Well, because it is the key to building rapport. If you develop rapport with others, things go your way, and opportunities present themselves. Rapport creates trust, and people gravitate to people they trust. If you have poor rapport, people will avoid you. Patients will be difficult to deal with, will fail appointments and will not comply with treatment, if you do not have rapport with them.

Promoting oral health using NLP

Visuals

Imagine you recognise that someone is visual by the words they use - like 'look', 'see', 'clear'. What you need to do is use those words yourself when you talk to the patient.

> "Imagine how bright your smile will be..."
> "Those veneers will make you look so much better..."
> "Your teeth are what people see when they look at you..."

Using words like this means that the patient will understand you more quickly and you're building rapport because, as well as giving information in a way they comprehend easily, you are communicating that you understand them. So, for visuals, stress all the positive benefits of oral health/treatment, which might affect how they look.

This is the art of utilising the principles of NLP - if you communicate with people in their preferred mode, you will accomplish much more than if you communicate in your own preferred mode.

When I was trying to get this book published, Stephen, the publisher, said things to me like: "I'd like to see how you see it shaping up. Can you give me a picture of the sort of book you want to do?"

To which I replied: "I want a bright, funny coloured cover, I want pictures and drawings, I want it to be really eye-catching, but the text very simple and clear."

And here you are, reading the book! I'm sure I'd have had to work much harder if Stephen hadn't been such an obviously visual thinker.

So for visual patients, use leaflets, photos, and draw pictures - (periodontal disease lends itself to this), and wave your hands about, paint pictures in the air. All this will quickly get visuals 'on-side'.

Auditories

Auditory patients may say things like:
> "Tell me how..."
> "What you are saying rings a bell."
> "That sounds okay."

And the trick is to try to use auditory verbal predicates back to them:

> "I hear what you are saying."
> "How does that sound?", etc.

Besides words, there are other auditory aids. Music in the surgery can be very useful. Music does affect emotions and behaviour. It conditions or soothes and auditory people are particularly sensitive to it.

The Muzak Corporation can increase factory output by 17%. Slow music in supermarkets raises sales by 30% because people walk more slowly and therefore buy more goods. If you ask people coming out of a supermarket about the music, 30% don't know what kind of music was on, and 40% will say there wasn't any, so music must work at an unconscious level.

Audiotapes are popular with auditories although brochures and leaflets are still useful, but you have to handle them differently than you would visuals.

For auditories, if you give them an information sheet, wait about twelve seconds, then explain it out loud. Twelve seconds allows them time to orient themselves and get a reference point - then they will want to hear it from you. They'll look along the top of the leaflet, down the left hand side and at a few things in the middle - but they won't try to read it or get information from it. After 12 seconds, they need you to explain what they just saw. This is different from visuals (who get more from seeing than from hearing). If you give them a sheet of information KEEP QUIET. Don't say anything until they renew eye contact.

Kinaesthetics

With kinaesthetics, you want to communicate with them in ways that directly relate to their feelings.

> "How do you feel about .....?"
> "How does that grab you?"

Also, give them things to touch, let them play with the floss, get them to feel what it's like when their oral hygiene is done properly – ask them to feel the toothbrush, feel the quality of the new crown.

If you give kinaesthetics leaflets just let them hold them. They will believe what you say about its contents because they can hold it, they can feel something concrete in their hands. Touching them and gesturing to them will also grab their attention.

Method of communication		Visuals	Auditories	Kinaesthetics
What words are used? (use these words when talking back to them)		See Look Show	Say Sound Tell Ring Hear	Feel Grab Touch
What do their eyes tell you?	I'm imagining/lying!	◉ ◉	◉ ◉	
	I'm remembering	◉ ◉	◉ ◉	
	I'm processing information, so don't speak to me for a minute!	◉ ◉ ahead, unfocussed		◉ ◉
How do you best communicate with this type?		Show pictures, photos, video, use your hands.	Use catchy phrases, music, tapes, explain written materials about 12 seconds after you give it to them.	Use props, models, things they can touch.

Listening skills

There are two other key elements in building and maintaining trust and rapport with patients. The first is listening and the second is non-verbal. Firstly, listening is an active process. It is not, as many think, a passive occupation. A good listener can shape the conversation as much as the speaker, but good listening involves a lot of mental hard work.

Many members of dental teams never really listen. Oral health personnel tend to talk and can actually put people off by 'overselling' oral health, and completely failing to listen to the person they are with (the patient). Have you ever been with someone (a partner perhaps) who looked at other people or things while you were talking and therefore appeared not to be listening to you. It is extremely annoying and it makes you want to slap them and say: 'pay attention'.

Listening is not easy. We can listen 10 times faster than we can talk. That's why it is difficult to do well because our minds race ahead and think about something else whilst the other person is talking.

There is a useful pneumonic which can be made from the letters of the word 'LISTEN':

L is for listening
I is for identifying main ideas
S is for speaking - but only ever when it's your turn
T is for thinking about what the other person is saying
E is for emotions and keeping them under control
N is for never changing the subject.

If you try to put these factors into your listening, you will probably realise how seldom you truly listen. You will also find that your ability to charm and influence is astonishingly enhanced.

More body language

Have you ever been in a crowded room, where no one can really hear anything that anyone says? If you watch people, they will drink when others drink, smile when others smile, laugh when others laugh, even though no one really knows what's being said. That is because, non-verbally, groups of people are building rapport.

Mirroring, or matching other people's body movements shows a high degree of rapport and it's also a technique that enhances trust. When two people enjoy each other's company, they come closer together, lean forward. If one crosses their legs, the other does too; if one fiddles with their specs, the other will pick up a pen and mirror the fiddling. They also match each other's tone and speed of speaking. It's as if they're trying to be more like each other, hoping to cut out all the differences - two people in love do a romantic dance, continually copying each other's movements.

People who don't like each other, or disagree with each other, mismatch. One will lean forward, the other back. One will put hands on hips, so the other puts them at their side. Adversaries will break eye contact. So watch your patient carefully, then after a few seconds, mirror what you see. You can sometimes do almost no talking, but will yet be highly persuasive because you have generated rapport. If you get rapport, you get trust. And if you get trust, you will get the patient's loyalty and compliance.

If you watch closely for matching and mismatching between you and the patient, you will see if you are connecting with them. If you say, or suggest something your patient doesn't like they will not match your movements - if things are going well, and they're following what you're saying, and liking it, they'll match you. So notice what your patient does and you'll be able to tell whether they're interested in what is being said.

Whether you like it or not, giving dental care implies a relationship. You need to know what your patient is communicating to you all the time you are with them. Once these things become second nature, you'll know exactly what to say to people and when to say it. You'll know when you are getting somewhere, and when to change what you are saying.

We guarantee if you practise all these techniques, your job (and your relationships) will become easier.

Below is a 'plan of action' to enable you to develop your NLP skills.

Day one:

Get people to describe things. Pick three friends and ask them to talk about:

- The town they grew up in
- Their family
- Their work.

Pick out their preferred mode of communication, just by listening to their words. After they've talked, ask them questions about what they've been describing. Ask:

- How they pictured the object/situation
- What sounds they remember
- What feelings come to mind.

Listen to the words they use and which they seem most comfortable with; picturing, remembering sounds, or how they feel. You can also ask them which they remembered best. Once you can spot the preferred mode of thinking of your friends, you will start to notice them in people at the surgery.

Day two:

Start watching eye movements.

Visual	up right (images of the future/imagining)
	up left (images of the past)
	unfocused (matching words to images)

Auditory	side right (sounds in the future/imagining sounds)
	side left (remembering sounds)
	down left (internal conversation)
Kinaesthetic	down right (accessing feelings)

Get someone to describe their dream house. Because they're thinking about the future, their eyes will move up right (visuals), side right (auditories) or down right (kinaesthetics). Then ask them to describe a house they remember. Their eyes will move up and left if they are thinking visually, directly left if thinking auditorially.

The point is that you get used to seeing what people look like when they access information. With patients, you need to be able to spot eye movements, and see whether the movements match what they're saying or doing. If they don't match - if they talk about the future and their eyes indicate they're talking about the past, you know something isn't right.

It is really worthwhile practising this because whatever role you play in your dental team or, indeed in life, learning to judge the truth of what you hear is a very useful trick.

Day three:

Practise listening, this will make you very popular. It will be very obvious to you, but people won't notice anything except that you are a thoroughly lovely person to be with.

Practise effective listening using the LISTEN pneumonic above.

Day four:

Think of a problem you have (work, home, partner). Then pick some friends and tell half of them the problem whilst copying their movements. Tell the other half without mirroring their movements. You will find that when you mirror the movements of the person you are talking to, they will be more attentive and will give more advice and encouragement.

Day five:

Watch how much people you talk to mirror you, then calibrate. When they mirror you, they like what you're saying, so keep going. When they don't like it they'll stop mirroring, so change your tack.

Day six:

Go to a party and use all that you have practised in the previous five days. You will be the most popular person there!

As stated at the beginning of this chapter, this description of some of the techniques of NLP is only a tiny part of the entirety of the subject. However, if you try the methods described, you will notice a transformation in your relationships with others and in your 'success' rates. It does take practice to become skilled with NLP methods, but it is an exciting journey and once you begin to trust the fact that these techniques really do enhance your life, you will be ready to tackle the more detailed and authoritative texts on the subject.

Further reading

Andreas S, Faulkner C. *NLP The New Technology of Achievement*. London: Nicholas Brealey Publishing Limited, 1996.

Jepsen CH. Neurolinguistic programming in dentistry. *J Calif Dent Ass* 1992 **20:** 28-32.

Johnson KL. *Selling with NLP*. London: Nightingale-Conant Corporation, 1993.

Walter J, Bayal A. Neurolinguistic programming. *Br Med J* 2003 **326:** 83, 133, 165-166.

Dealing with Problems

7

*"It isn't that they can't see the solution,
it is that they can't see the problem"*

G K Chesterton
The Point of a Pin

Despite a dental team's best efforts, from time to time you will encounter problems in your relationships with each other and with patients, and you may find this somewhat difficult to deal with. This chapter offers the theoretical background underlying how such circumstances (which might be extremely stressful) may be understood and dealt with.

Spotting problems before they start

The most important step in avoiding problems in the surgery is to reduce anxiety as much as possible. Developing the ability to spot anxiety, discomfort, depression or anger, and if possible, doing so before those feelings have been expressed or acknowledged by the patient is therefore important. Thus, being aware of clues can help you to divert an encounter away from a poor outcome. These clues might involve reduced eye contact (anxiety), slow hesitant speech (anxiety, depression), contraction of pupils (pain, discomfort), crossed limb positions (defensiveness), prolonged eye contact (aggression), inappropriate responses (confusion, anxiety), clenching of hands or chair arms (anxiety). Thus, the entire dental team must constantly be on the look-out for signs which indicate potential problems, and, on spotting such signs must take immediate action to circumvent further trouble. Being alert for signs of anxiety is a good start, the next step is taking specific and appropriate action in order to deal with the anxiety.

It is important to realise that anxiety about dentistry may be quite reasonable. Patients have real and legitimate cause for concern about whether their teeth will need to be extracted, whether the treatment they receive will be painful or uncomfortable and whether they will be able to pay the bill once the treatment is complete.

Also, the very fact that the person is not in their usual environment but in a dental surgery can arouse long-buried fears, and will often stimulate unpleasant memories of traumatic dental experiences. The anxiety that is engendered might cause the patient to be irritable, or perhaps attention-seeking and demanding. Equally, anxious patients may act in a withdrawn way. This withdrawal stems from patients erecting psychological barriers around themselves. Until someone gains their trust, they will be unable to break through these barriers and share their worries. To gain this trust, and to calm down an excited patient, you need to let them know that you are aware of their feelings, for example, "you look rather worried."

You might then continue by asking the patient the precise cause of their worry:

> "What is it that bothers you particularly?"

This will further reassure the patient because the line of questioning lets them know that, not only do you know how they feel, but also, that you are prepared to take specific actions and make particular efforts to alleviate their anxiety. It is NOT helpful to say:

> "Come on now, don't worry."
>   OR
> "Just relax."

Such comments merely suggest to the patient that you do not understand their worries, think them rather silly and have no intention whatever of taking their anxieties into account during your treatment planning or while the treatment is being carried out. The team should listen quietly to an anxious patient and encourage him or her to talk about whatever is uppermost in their mind. This will make the patient feel accepted, that an interest has been taken and that someone is at least trying to understand his or her worries.

Asking the patient specifically how you might help them to feel more comfortable can be extremely calming. Firstly, to do so tells the patient that they are the expert on their own feelings; secondly, you might get some extremely useful tips, and thirdly it empowers the patient and enhances their feelings of control.

Finally, the provision of accurate and simple explanations of whatever is to be done often helps to reduce some of the patient's worries. Often, fantasies and horror stories about dentistry have given patients erroneous ideas about what is likely to happen to them.

How do people deal with their own anxiety?

All of us, on occasions, deceive ourselves in order that we can see things as we would prefer to see them. These defence mechanisms are there so that we can protect ourselves from feelings with which we are unable to cope. All members of the dental team, and certainly many anxious patients will use these mechanisms from time to time. Some are useful and constructive whilst others may be destructive.

Sublimation

This mechanism translates powerful and unacceptable urges into behaviours that are socially permitted. For example, the dental nurse who names the squash ball after the practice manager provides an example of sublimation. It is definitely better that she hits the squash ball rather than the manager and vigorous physical activity actually does reduce interpersonal aggression.

Compensation

People with some disability develop high levels of skills in other spheres. For example, a girl who regards herself as unattractive may develop a particularly winning personality. However, compensatory behaviours can also engender difficulties. The patient who feels particularly powerless in the surgery may behave in an abusive and dictatorial manner in order to compensate for their feelings of helplessness.

Activity

People sometimes deal with their anxiety by distracting themselves with other activities. The anxious person will keep busy and occupy him or herself. This may be seen as a fidgety chattering patient.

Rationalisation

Rationalisation is mentioned in Chapter 5 and helps us to invent reasons for doing things when we know in our hearts that we should not do them. It also helps us to allow ourselves to fail to reach the goals we have set ourselves.

Patients (and members of the team) who indulge in excessive rationalisation of their actions are unlikely to learn anything when things go wrong, as they will deceive themselves that they had adequate reasons for behaving as they did, even if a poor outcome resulted.

"It was okay for me to be rude to that patient, they deserved it. It wasn't my fault they've made a complaint about the practice."

Withdrawal

Sometimes situations are so frightening that people will remove themselves physically. This is a classic reaction to dentistry. Patients who find the whole prospect too daunting simply do not attend. A withdrawal action may of course be psychological rather than the simple physical absence. Patients who have had their trust and faith in dentists betrayed will be extremely cautious about trusting any dentist in the future.

Various other defence mechanisms exist. All involve a degree of distortion of the facts and self-deception. However, we all use them in almost all our interpersonal behaviours. There is no simple solution for a dental team dealing with difficult patients. Neurotic behaviour, stress during visits and anxiety are all genuine. Blaming the patient, telling them to behave differently, or worse, simply avoiding and rejecting such patients will only make their problems worse. What is vital is that the team try to understand their patients' behaviours.

Below is one method that you can use to help you to understand your interactions with patients, other staff members, friends and family. Basically it rests upon the idea that every personality is made up of three components - the parent, the adult and the child. Put simply, which of these 'surfaces' during a conversation or interplay between two people, is crucial to how the two people relate to each other.

Adopting roles

In every situation in which we are placed, we play different roles. For example, you will behave differently when you are relaxing with friends than when you are asking your bank manager for a loan. However, it is important to realise that the type of role adopted by one person will affect the role adopted by the other person in an encounter. Whether the roles played by each person add up to a satisfactory or unsatisfactory interplay between the participants depends on the role chosen by each.

We all have three "ego states" which we can adopt. Which one we choose depends upon many factors but one of the most important influences is the ego state of the other participant in the relationship. The three ego states which are internal to all of us and which affect our relationships are the 'parent', the 'child' and the 'adult'.

The parent ego state

The ego state in which the "do as I say" attitude is taken (the 'parent' ego state) is often the one adopted by dental teams. It can be a caring role: "this is best for you", but can lead to problems for two reasons:

- If we wish to empower people to take care of their own health, this guiding, sometimes paternalistic approach is counterproductive

- If patients do not want to be like a passive child and wish instead to behave in an adult role, a crossed "transaction" leading to poor communication will result.

The adult ego state

The rational decision maker, who offers reasons and choices for each course of action is named the adult ego state. It is sometimes difficult for the dental team to adopt this role because the patient has adopted a 'child' ego state and appears to want to be guided and 'parented', thus forcing the dental team into 'parent' ego state. However, if the dental professionals adopt the rational adult ego state, they will encourage the adoption of an 'adult' role by the patient. This is the ego state most likely to result in improved oral health because this is the ego state which accepts responsibility and makes 'good', evidence-based decisions. A patient is more likely to take up a new set of behaviours because he wants to and has chosen to, than because he has been told it will be 'good' for him. We want, therefore, as far as possible, to relate to the patient's adult ego state.

The child ego state

The ego state which responds to authority and power, by doing as it is told, or by being cross and frustrated, is the child ego state. Many patients will adopt their child ego state when visiting the dentist (largely, we suspect, because they have been 'trained' to do so, because health care professionals so often adopt parental ego states). As mentioned above, although parent-child interactions might lead to acquiescent patients, they are not likely to lead to successful health choices. It is also a role that is increasingly being challenged by patients as they begin to recognise the importance of their own lifestyles and choices to their own health.

Roles in the dental surgery

As a member of the dental team, perhaps the easiest (but not the best) role to adopt is that of a parent. By doing so, in actual fact, our attitude will appear to the patient to be one of:

"I know best, therefore you ought to do as I say."

Taking on this 'parent' ego state will only lead to successful relationships with patients if they are prepared to play a somewhat 'child-like' role, which accepts that you are more powerful and have all the responsibility for their health care.

An alternative role which the health care professional might play is that of a rational decision maker by taking care that their 'adult' ego state surfaces during the encounter. For example:

"This, I believe, is the best course of action because of x, y, z."

Whether dropping the parent role and taking on an adult ego state will lead to successful relationships between team and patient will again depend on whether the patient will also adopt a rational, reasoning, participatory role. If they prefer to adopt a passive role and adopt a child ego state:

"Oh, I don't know what's best, you're the dentist, you choose."

the interaction may become fraught and difficult, with the patient losing faith in your ability to 'guide' them in the right direction, i.e. the patient becomes an 'orphaned' child. This happens because the second participant (the patient) is not responding in the role in which they were addressed (their adult ego state). It is not 'wrong' for them to do so, but a crossed interaction (parent to adult, or adult to child) will lead to poor communication.

Therefore, to avoid conflict, the dental team need to assess whether the patient wishes to act in a participatory manner, or a passive manner. However, since health is likely to be enhanced by patients taking responsibility for their own health, wherever possible, the dental team should attempt to encourage mutual rational participation in treatment rather than simply giving guidance and expecting cooperation, i.e. both patient and professional should ideally be functioning in their adult ego state.

Below is a series of potential areas of conflict within the dental surgery. Each attempts to illustrate 'successful' and 'crossed' transactions between the participants.

Dental attendance

Patient: "It's rather difficult for me to come next Thursday, I've got to see an old friend."
(Adult to Adult)

Receptionist: "Well, if your social life means you can't come, so be it."
(Parent to Child)

In this transaction, the patient acted as an equal (an adult ego state), offering a reason for their possible non-attendance (although why should they feel that they have to do this since they are the customer) and was met by a judgemental (parental ego state) response, which in effect tells the patient that they are acting irresponsibly. If there really is no alternative appointment, the receptionist, by treating the patient as an equal, could at least respond in a more reasonable fashion. For example:

Receptionist: "I'm afraid we just don't have any other appointments. Would it be possible to alter your arrangement?" (Adult to Adult)

Non-cooperation with advice

Dentist: "You haven't been taking your denture out at night like I told you to, have you." (Parent to Child)

Patient: "Well no, I haven't, I find it too embarrassing." (Adult to Adult)

Dentist: "Well you have to, else you'll lose the rest of your teeth." (Parent to Child)

Here the dentist has adopted an air of 'you're naughty, you didn't obey me'. Had he taken time to explain the precise reasoning for nighttime denture removal, and acknowledged the patient's problems with doing so, some compromise might have been reached. As this crossed transaction stands, the patient is highly unlikely to do as the dentist has instructed, because it seems like an unjustified 'order' rather than an action which is being suggested for the patient's benefit. The situation will be likely to cause dismay and frustration unless the patient adopts a child ego state, for example:

"Okay, you're the boss, I'll leave it out." (Child to Parent)

However, although this would resolve the current dilemma and the patient agrees to do as the dentist suggests, forcing a patient into this role increases their passivity and this decreases their ability to make health choices when they are alone.

An alternative way in which the interaction can be prevented from being a failure would be if the dentist as well as the patient adopted an adult ego state, such as:

"You see, your mouth gets drier at night, and so bacteria grow which can damage your gums and remaining teeth." (Adult to Adult)

You may be thinking here: "Well, how do I tell my patients that their mouth is still dirty without seeming to criticise them and thereby thrusting them into a child ego state?" The key to successful transactions is to broach the subject, ensuring that you have adopted a non-judgemental adult ego state, as in:

Hygienist   "How are you getting on with the new toothbrush?"
                   (Adult to Adult)

Patient (a)   "Well, I've tried. But I just can't seem to reach the back teeth."
                   (Adult to Adult)

OR

Patient (b)   "Hopeless. I just can't do it. I've tried and I can't manage."
                   (Child to Parent)

At this point, the hygienist must respond appropriately. For patient (a) an adult ego state response is required, with careful explanation and a rational approach to the problem. For patient (b), a supportive parental-type response is necessary in order to avoid a crossed transaction:

Hygienist: "I'm sure you are making a difference. We'll go over it again and see what's bothering you".
                   (Parent to Child)

Hopefully by transferring the responsibility for detecting and rectifying the problems to the patient, they will be encouraged to adopt an adult ego state. This, as mentioned before, it is the state most conducive to both learning, and sustained behaviour change.

Non-cooperation with treatment

Provided that treatment planning proceeds with both parties in adult ego states, with appropriate explanations of what is involved in a course of treatment and in the aftercare at home, it is rare for non-cooperation to occur.

Non-cooperation with treatment (other than in children) suggests that either:

The treatment plan has been decided by the clinician (in parent ego state) according to what was thought best for the patient.

OR

Although the patient in partnership with the clinician has seemed to have chosen a particular treatment option, the explanations about what would be involved were insufficient (again, often due to adoption of a parental ego state by the clinician).

Negative attitudes to treatment results

Negative attitudes to the results of treatment are usually due to unduly high expectations on the part of the patient. Again, ensuring full participation by the patient at the treatment planning stage should avoid such problems. The preliminary discussions must include descriptions of untoward (poor) treatment outcomes, as well as details of the (hoped for) good outcomes, plus the best possible estimate of how likely these outcomes are (see Chapter 10).

Dentist   "If I fit a crown on this tooth, there is a small possibility that it will not stand up to your bite, and may fracture. In that case we would have to extract the root. But that possibility is pretty unlikely."
                (Adult to Adult)
                                OR

Dentist   "A crown there will look super. Yes, I think that would be best."
                (Parent to Child)

If things do go wrong, can the patient with the second dentist truly be said to have given informed consent, and can anyone really blame them for feeling aggrieved if the dentist's predictions do not come true? Treatment failures will be accepted by patients if a rational explanation of why they occur has been given at the outset. In difficult cases, it is absolutely vital that an adult-to-adult transaction has taken place during the treatment planning stage *(see Chapter 10)*.

Non-payment of fees

This too is an area, which so long as everything has been agreed at the outset of treatment, should not cause problems. However, there will be occasions when non-payment does become a problem. This usually occurs if the fee is more than the patient expected to pay, and hence is indicative of poor communication at some point during the treatment. It is best to discuss fees in positive terms, which encourage positive answers:

> "The fee for your treatment today is £50."

This communicates to the patient that the payment is expected today. Whilst if the receptionist says:

> "The fee is £50. Would you like to pay now, or shall we put it on a bill?"

the intimation to the patient is that it is not important that they pay promptly. This may discourage future good relationships between practice and patient as statements must then be sent in order to collect the money. It is much easier for patients to appreciate the value for money which they are getting, if they are parting with their cash at a time close to completion of treatment rather than weeks later.

Most importantly, team members should never argue with patients. Patients who are aggressive or argumentative have a problem, which should be met with a solution. Therefore, if patients are facing financial hardships, let them know that you can organise a method of payment which will help the to meet their obligations. When dealing with non-paying patients, the team members must, in adult ego state, attempt to find out whether the patient was satisfied with the:

- Way they were treated at the practice (generally)
- Dental treatment they received
- Explanation regarding fees that preceded that treatment
- Outcomes of treatment.

Once a patient recognises, through such a discussion, that they have no reason not to pay, then the problem is usually resolved. Before blaming the patient for non-payment, the dental team should ensure that the patient knows, not only how much to pay, but to whom, how the money should be paid, when the money should be paid and whether the practice run any financial plans for those faced with large bills.

Confrontation and negotiation

Inevitably there will be times when members of the dental team will become angry. We all, on occasions, find ourselves in conflict with others, or believe that someone else is being destructive. A committed dental team will risk confronting each other when there is a problem in order that the destructive patterns of behaviour do not continue.

Resolving conflicts within a dental practice requires that a number of steps are taken.

Step 1 Confront the confrontation

The first step towards improving a bad situation is for someone to express their views about the problem and to encourage other people to do so. The aim of this step is to explore the problem and the feelings and needs of the participants.

Confronting the issue will bring about some resolution of the conflict if there is a true 'team' approach within the practice and if the person being confronted is confident and able to change.

An important point. If you wish to confront a problem, do not do so when everyone is busy and there is no time to discuss and negotiate. Hit and run tactics will escalate conflicts and build anger and resentment.

Step 2 Decide what you are arguing about

Once you have confronted someone about something, the next step is to make sure that all parties understand the reason for the conflict. Care must be taken to be specific, and not to describe each other in ways that insult. Instead:

Step 3 Communicate feelings

The idea here is for all participants to understand how their thoughts, feelings and needs differ from each other.

Step 4 Tell them you are willing to take action to resolve the conflict

In order to reach agreement when you are trying to find a way to resolve conflict, it is essential that you express how willing you are to cooperate.

Step 5 Trying on others' shoes

Resolving conflicts requires that you make serious efforts to understand the other people involved. Therefore, you must listen to what they say and try to take up their perspective. Role playing can be useful here. Try to present the other person's point of view in order to give you insight into their viewpoint.

Step 6 Reaching agreement

Conflict ends when people agree on a set of actions which all are happy with.

Steps to Resolving Conflict

(1)   What is the **real** problem?
(2)   What are the key issues upsetting people?
(3)   How do you all feel about the problem?
(4)   Will we do anything about it?
(5)   How does the other person feel?
(6)   What shall we do about it?

Final thoughts

This chapter has introduced the concept of transactional analysis and negotiation when there is conflict. Familiarity with the verbal and non-verbal cues and clues which are detailed in Chapter 3 and the skills described in Chapter 6 can help the dental team to identify the problems which their patients are expressing. It is also essential for members of the dental team to be able to recognise their own and each other's ego states. Doing so will enhance communication between members of the team and thus make it more likely that crossed transactions between themselves and with patients are avoided.

Also, it should be clear by now that, although for years dentistry has taken a 'parenting' role, to do so is counter productive. Casting each patient as a helpless child will do exactly that - turn them into helpless, reliant children. Thus the team's aim should be adult-to-adult communication throughout their practice. This, of course, implies that all participants - that is all members of the team, and all patients, must view each other as equals. For some people this is a difficult thing to do.

The public have for many years deferred to dentists and health carers as figures of authority who command respect. Because of this, many patients do not feel powerful enough in the dental environment to participate in decisions or adopt their adult ego state. It is sometimes extremely difficult to develop one's relationship with a patient to the point whereby they will share in the decisions made in the practice - but unless considerable efforts are made to do this, we are using our power to teach helplessness rather than self-care. And as has been said many times before in this book, what a patient does at home on a day-to-day basis has far, far more to do with the state of their oral health than any actions taken within the surgery.

Finally, our society is becoming increasingly litigious. Research has shown that poor relationships with health care providers and feelings of not being kept informed, play a powerful role in people's decisions to take legal advice about health care received. Thus, improving relationships with patients and being able to analyse our interactions with them is important, even for the less altruistic of the profession. Transaction before action should be the watchword. Telling people what they want is no longer appropriate.

Further reading

Bailey J, Baille L. Transactional analysis: how to improve communication skills. *Nurs Stand* 1996 **10**: 39-42.

Caraher M. Nursing and health education: victim blaming. *Br J Nurs* 1995 4: 1190-1192, 1209-1213.

Elaad E. Detection of deception: a transactional analysis perspective. *J Psychol* 1993 **127**: 5-15.

Mackay RT. Transactional analysis applied to family living. *Health Educ* 1986 **17**: 37.

Assertiveness without Aggression

8

"That which seems most feeble and bewildered in you is the strongest and most determined"

Kahil Gibran.
The Prophet. 1926

Introduction

Every now and then situations may arise in the surgery that require a member of the dental team to deal with a patient in an assertive manner. A word of caution: assertive is NOT a synonym for aggressive and, no matter how angry, frustrated or out of control you might feel, aggression will always be counter productive and is likely to increase, rather than reduce, the feelings of tension. Assertiveness does not mean being hard-nosed, bullying, self-centred or hostile. It is also not something that only the shy and retiring should know about. Those of us who are naturally 'bolshy' can benefit enormously from learning to be assertive, as aggression and energy can become more productively used if the principles of assertiveness are adhered to.

The need to be assertive stems from the power relations that often exist between two individuals. Almost invariably, when one person is dealing with another, one of the two parties has more power, or a higher status than the other. In fact, we become so used to this arrangement (parent-child, teacher-pupil, dentist-patient, employer-employee) that we forget that power need not be divided so unequally. It is not necessary for interactions between individuals to be based on the 'top-dog' and 'under-dog', powerful and powerless principle. There is a middle path and it is this principle of equality which is the key to assertiveness and successful communication, especially under difficult circumstances.

> Assertiveness involves standing up for legitimate rights and communicating our needs, wants, feelings and beliefs in direct, honest and appropriate ways without violating the rights of others.

The hallmark of being assertive is that each party in an exchange can pass on messages about what they think, how they feel and how they see the situation without dominating or degrading the other individual. From this definition, it is clear that, for a dental team to function well, both for and with patients, assertiveness from all (especially the patients) is required and should be encouraged.

To be an assertive dental professional, two types of respect are needed. Firstly, respect for oneself and secondly (but just as importantly) respect for others. This recognition of the rights of others is important as, contrary to popular opinion, assertiveness is not a means of getting what one wants, or controlling or manipulating others. The goal, when being assertive and encouraging others in the surgery to do so, is simply open and direct communication and that is the reason for the inclusion of the subject in this text. The aim is to ensure that both parties' needs are at least partially met. Thus, others have as much right to be assertive as you do (although not aggressive).

Below are some examples that have occurred in dental surgeries. They are chosen to illustrate the different forms which assertiveness can take.

The receptionist

Sue, recently appointed as a second receptionist in a very busy town-centre surgery, was absolutely thrilled with her luck in landing such a well-paid, convenient and challenging job. Her boss had verbally told her that, although she should take a lunch break between 1.00 p.m. and 2.00 p.m. each day, he had also hinted that, on occasions she may be required to miss some of her breaks. He had suggested that if such a scenario arose, she would be given time off in lieu. During the first week, on two occasions Sue had had only 15 minutes lunch break and had not yet been offered any extra time off. In her second week at work, she was looking forward to having lunch with her mother, whom she seldom saw, and who just happened to be passing through the town. Just before 1.00 p.m., the practice manager handed her some urgent work and asked her, as a favour, to work through her lunch hour. She unhappily cancelled her lunch date and put on a brave face, not wanting to make a fuss in this new job, which she was so pleased to have landed.

Sue's problem was that if she insisted on taking her lunch hour, she would cause conflict to herself because her loyalties to the job and to her mother were at odds with each other. An important aspect of assertive behaviour is that it allows negotiation when there is a conflict of priorities. In this case, a possible solution might have been for Sue to explain the importance of her lunchtime arrangements. She could also use the situation to remind the boss of his promises and suggest that, just as she was to have time off in lieu for extra hours worked, on this occasion she would be happy to turn that arrangement round. Sue could offer to stay late in the evening to finish the lunchtime work. Thus, a compromise that met everyone's objectives could have been achieved.

The nurse-receptionist

Working in an all male practice, Stella, a very attractive nurse-receptionist, who did her utmost to make patients feel happy and comfortable, felt that a desperately difficult situation had arisen. One particular male patient persisted, each time he came to the surgery, in patting her bottom and putting an arm round her shoulders whilst making suggestive comments. What she wanted to do was to slap the patient's face and tell him to get lost, particularly because he was an ugly little worm! Although this would have made her feel a lot better, it would have lost the practice a valued patient and probably disrupted the entire surgery. After suffering for two visits, on the third visit Stella turned to face the patient, told him, without being abusive or raising her voice (or hand!) that she found the behaviour unacceptable and demanded that he would not indulge in the behaviour again, either with herself or anyone else. She made it clear that the man's behaviour was offensive. It worked; and from that day, the gentleman treated Stella with utmost respect.

The patient

Samson's eleven-year-old daughter was suffering from repeated earache for which no cause could be found by the child's doctor. In desperation, the doctor referred the child to Mr. Owen, a local dental practitioner. Samson's anxiety and desire for a diagnosis made him aggressive when Mr. Owen explained that the black staining in the fissures of a posterior tooth was definitely not the cause of the child's discomfort. The dentist's desperation to help the child and to calm the aggressive father resulted in him opening the tooth, against his better judgement, even though he was convinced that no symptoms could possibly be being experienced from the tooth.

Mr. Owen had allowed himself to be pressurised by Samson's aggression. He needed to maintain his confidence about his own expertise even under pressure. Samson, whose anxiety made him deaf to reason, did not treat the dentist as an equal but as someone to be coerced into action, pointless though that action was.

Basic rights

It is sensible here to consider some basic rights applicable to all people. It is helpful in difficult situations, which require non-aggressive assertion, to remember these rights.

1. Despite any role which you take on (as part of the dental team, or as wife, mother, father, employee) it is important to remind yourself that you also have a right to have, and to state, your personal needs and priorities. This does not imply that you no longer have to honour the responsibilities inherent in your daily life but that you have needs that are separate from those of the people around you.

2. Your knowledge, expertise and capabilities give you a right to be treated as an equal. Some patients cast the dental team as people whose role is all-powerful, whilst others regard health workers as beings whose only responsibility is to serve their needs. As a member of a dental team, you are neither of these things. Respect your own intelligence and common sense but do not allow yourself to assume you have either more, or less, of either of these attributes than the patients who visit the surgery.

3. You have a right to feel what you feel and to express yourself. Often, by explaining your feelings in a reasoned and appropriate way, you will feel less urge to shout, scream, walk out or cry. If you suppress how you feel, for example, about the way in which children are treated in the surgery, because you believe that you will be judged as being over sentimental, or 'soft', you will become upset. Even if your values are different from the rest of the team, you still have a right to respect and express your own judgements.

4. You have a right to make your own choices. You do not have to justify your actions. For example, a dentist who decides to take a postgraduate qualification may feel that the decision must be justified by such comments as "because it will be a practice builder" or "because it will help me to undertake new types of treatment". No further justification than "because I want to" is needed.

5. Making mistakes is acceptable. People sometimes do silly stupid things. This does not mean that the person is silly or stupid. When you make a mistake or things do not go as planned, it does not indicate that there is an intrinsic flaw in your being or personality. The ability to admit to ourselves when we make mistakes, without it destroying our belief in ourselves, is crucially important to our ability to behave and communicate assertively.

6. You can change your mind. Refusing to alter a plan of action and proceeding with a commitment you are unhappy with can be a reflection that you made a decision for the wrong reasons. If you change your mind about something, it is not an indication that you are a whimsical butterfly, incapable of making decisions.

7. Often we feel shame and embarrassment when we do not understand something. It is important for those who wish to learn to become more assertive, to realise that you can no more be expected to know everything about everything than you can expect to be perfect! You are not being ridiculous if you ask for more information or a repeated explanation.

8. Everyone has a right to ask for what they want. Patients have a right to ask it of the dental team and, equally, the dental team has a right to ask it of patients. The same rules apply within the dental team. For example, the dentist has a right to ask for extra help from the staff if he needs it. Equally, dental nurses have a right to ask dentists to write legibly if their scrawl is making their job difficult.

9. A very important right, which is further alluded to in Chapter 11, is that we all have a right to decline responsibility for others. This does not mean that patients' welfare does not come first, but simply that, because the team have built a relationship with a patient, this does not mean that they have to take on the responsibility for the patient's overall well-being. It is important for each of the team to set limits concerning which of their patients' needs should be put before their own, and which should not. For example, although the team might decide that it is their responsibility to offer emergency care at the end of a busy day to a child in pain, they cannot offer an open-all-hours service for people who simply wish their dental care to fit with their own convenience.

10. Lastly, and perhaps most importantly, none of us is dependent on others

for approval. We cannot expect all patients to think we are fabulous. The need to be liked and approved of is extremely powerful but it is important, if assertive behaviour is to be the norm in the surgery, to learn that the world will not come to an end if you are not accepted and approved of by everyone, all of the time.

Check list for assertiveness

1. Respect your own needs and priorities
2. We are all equals
3. Your feelings are legitimate and should be expressed
4. You have a right to make your own choices
5. Everyone makes mistakes
6. Changing your mind is OK
7. You can't know everything
8. Ask for what you want
9. You cannot be responsible for everyone
10. It doesn't matter if everyone doesn't like you.

Techniques for assertiveness

There are three major skills that you need to enable you to be assertive.

- It is vital that you are DIRECT and SPECIFIC about what you want or feel

- Stick to your guns! If necessary, repeat your statement about what you want/feel, over and over again.

- Look out for ways in which people might try to undermine your assertiveness. If you are not aware of these tactics, you will be sidetracked.

Specificity

This is the art of stating precisely what you want to say, without any frills or furbelows! Frequently, we 'dress up' what we wish to say with unnecessary and extra words. This is particularly likely when feelings of anxiety are high, usually the times when we most need to be assertive.

Patient   "I'm very sorry, I'm always getting dates muddled, but I won't be able to come for my appointment next week."

Here the patient simply wishes to let you know that he cannot attend for an appointment. Why did he not simply say "I can't make my appointment on the 24th."?

OR

Receptionist: "I wondered if we were going to be busy next Wednesday. I, er, have to have the washing machine fixed. I know I shouldn't ask, but, would it be possible for me to have the afternoon off?"

With the unnecessary padding removed, this longwinded statement translates to:

"I'd like next Wednesday afternoon off. Would that be possible?"

The key to being specific is to decide exactly what it is that you want to express and stick to that single point without clouding the issue by adding other information. Using preambles and circumlocution only serves to weaken your statement. It also prevents the listener from understanding quickly what you want.

You are much more likely to get what you want if you are direct and specific. It is insufficient to assume that people (even those who are closest to us) will automatically understand us and empathise with our feelings. It is easier for people to respond to explicit requests, than to hints, sighs or complaints. People (especially anxious patients) are not telepathic - you must therefore give clear statements of what is required.

Sticking to your guns

Once you have determined what you wish to say and have found a way of making your statement clearly, specifically and directly, you must then stick to it. Even if your statement is met by a torrent of abuse, or a request is met by a blank refusal, you will need to repeat what you have said, without getting angry or raising your voice. Simply keep saying what you wish to say until you get a response and you believe the other party to have understood you.

Although anger may be one reaction you might receive, the other person, in order to deflect you from your point and thereby avoid respecting your wishes, may use other tactics. The commonest of these are:

- Manipulative comment
- Irrelevant logic
- Argumentative bait.

Receptionist	"Mr. Smith, we sent you an account last month and it has still not been settled".
Mr. Smith	"Oh yes, I was away on holiday last month." (Irrelevant logic)
Receptionist	"I hope you had a nice time but the account must be settled, Mr. Smith."
Mr. Smith	"You lot, always after money, ripping us all off you are." (Argumentative bait)
Receptionist	"Since the work in your mouth is complete, you must settle your bill, Mr. Smith".
Mr. Smith	"Well I'm bringing my wife in for treatment next week. Another customer for you." (Manipulative comment)
Receptionist	"We'll be starting a new account then, but this one must be settled today."

Mr. Smith grumpily pulls out his credit card.

Note that, where possible, the receptionist commented on the patient's statement. It is important that you do not simply keep saying the same thing over and over again, without acknowledging or responding to the other person. If you sound like a record that has stuck, you will not be assertive, but at the same time you should not allow yourself to be sidetracked.

Don't be undermined

Although you need to indicate that you have heard what the other person has said, it is important not to lose track of your point. You must maintain your statement. In the hypothetical responses below the first half of the sentence acknowledges what has been said, but the second half assertively states what is required.

"You may never have paid this much before, but the account must be settled."

"I understand that you wish to come on a Saturday, but there are no free appointments that day."

"I realise that we will be busy this evening, but I am not working late tonight."

"I know you have fewer patients on your list, but I feel I deserve a pay rise."

"Perhaps you do like the idea of white fillings, but amalgam will not make you ill."

"I know your mouth feels uncomfortable, but there is not a piece of tooth left in the socket."

Making the most of criticism

There will be times during your working life when you will be criticised. Sometimes this will be justifiable criticism and on other occasions criticisms are no more than insults, designed to aggravate you.

To deal with criticism assertively, we first need to distinguish between criticism which is valid, criticism which is invalid and the simple put-down, insult or 'wind-up'.

Valid criticism

Imagine that you know that you have arrived late, done a job badly, forgotten to pass on a message. If your action (or lack of it) is commented upon, you need to take it on the chin. There is fact in what is being said and you were the person involved. But, it is not necessary to dissolve into abject and grovelling apology, nor is it productive to be cross. The most assertive way in which valid criticism can be dealt with is acknowledging the truth in what the critic says.

>"Yes, it was me who forgot to send those impressions to the lab."

and, if you truly are sorry, an apology can be added.

>"I've left all today's patients' notes at home. I know that's going to cause us all problems, I'm very sorry."

However, if someone criticises you for something you rather like about yourself, you should not apologise. Imagine someone criticised you for holding up the smooth running of the surgery by chatting too long to your patients. If you rather like your relationship with the patients, don't say:

>"Yes, I know, I talk too much, I'm ever so sorry."

but be assertive by acknowledging the valid criticism but at the same time by being honest.

>"Yes, I do talk a lot to them all, but I like it, I think it helps them to relax here."

Invalid criticism/put-down

If someone says something that is not true, the fact that they have said it does not make it any more accurate. If someone makes an invalid criticism of you, you need to grasp the bull by the horns and refute the comment absolutely.

>"That is untrue."
>"That isn't right."
>"I don't accept that."

For example:

Patient   "The work you've done in my mouth is shoddy. It's not up to standard."

Dentist   "I do not accept that at all. My work is always of the highest standard."

Whatever reply this response engenders, remember to stick to your guns and repeat as often as you wish, that you do not accept the criticism.

Acknowledging why the criticism has been made, even though it is not true, may also be useful.

Nurse   "You're always moaning at me or being horrid."

Dentist   "That is not true. I get bossy when I'm stressed, but I'm not always horrid."

Always begin with refuting the statement. Don't give your explanation first as it may come out sounding like an excuse.

Patient   "You've messed it up. You sent me a card saying Friday and here I am and there's no dentist."

Receptionist   "But I always put a record in the book when I send out a card. I haven't messed it up."

A more assertive response would be:

"That's not right. I always put a record in the book when I send a card."

Last thoughts

In essence, the ability to be assertive is based in self-esteem and it therefore enables us to relate to others in an entirely new way. It is very important that assertiveness does not become confused with selfishness. Assertiveness requires that we consider how others are affected by our remarks and that we consider their wants and needs whilst at the same time remaining honest about ours. Assertiveness can improve your relationships with everyone around you because if all are assertive, then everything is clear and everyone is honest.

Repeatedly practising the skills of assertiveness in the dental surgery will make the whole concept become more and more important. Instead of feeling confident about handling certain specific situations, you will become generally more confident and assertive. Adopting assertiveness techniques leads to being more open and more relaxed, exactly the ambience that promotes good communication. Changing a dental practice into one where equality reigns and direct, honest communication occurs at all times is an enormous challenge and will take hard work and commitment, but is definitely worthwhile for both staff and patients.

Further reading

Atkinson HG. Are you a 'good' patient? Yes – if you're courteously assertive. *Health News* 2003 **9**: 5.

Boswell S. Building the dental dream team: behavioural styles in practice. *J Contemp Dent Pract* 2000 **15**: 76-85.

Freeman LH, Adams PF. Comparative effectiveness of two training programmes on assertive behaviour. *Nurs Stand* 1999 **13**: 32-35.

Schill J. Self-defeating personality, argumentativeness and assertive self-statements. *Psychol Rep* 1996 **79**: 1103-1106.

Children - Special Cases

9

*"Children do not give up their innate imagination,
curiosity, dreaminess, easily. You have to love
them to get them to do that".*

R D Laing

Introduction

This separate chapter about communicating effectively with children emphasises that the younger patient should not simply be treated like a "mini" version of the older one. Children's life experiences, and their expectations, are completely different to those of the adult and therefore dental teams need to make special efforts for their child patients.

Attracting a number of children to a practice and forming a good relationship while they are still young ensures that their health can be maintained and healthy habits established early. It also means that a group of confident, loyal and dentally aware patients are assured for the practice's future years. People who happily attend a dentist regularly as children tend to do so as adults, and most will remain with their childhood practice, unless they leave the area. Time and effort spent with children now is therefore a good investment for the future. Many clinical texts discuss 'child management' in the dental surgery as if the overall objective is simply to find a way in which (apparently dangerously disruptive) small people can be persuaded to submit to dental treatment.

However, just as for adult patients, the aim should be to encourage children to feel that their teeth are important to them. It is much more likely that this will be the outcome if the child enjoys a trip to the practice, rather than finding it a terrifying ordeal.

How are children different?

Apart from the obvious size difference between children and adults there are other more important differences, which, if they are understood by the dental team, will help to ensure that the rapport between the practice and its child patients is as good as the rapport the team have with the adult patients.

Many members of the dental team will be familiar and at ease with children, having had experiences either of their own, or through dealing with the children of relatives and friends. However, for those who have hitherto not had close contact with future generations, the table below lists a few of the developmental landmarks which a child will go through.

Table 9.1

Age (years)	Suggestions
0 - 2	Avoid separation from parent Physical support required Restrict vocabulary to appropriate level
2 - 4	Choose imaginative words Appeal to fantasy Accept swings between very positive acceptance and rejection Child may: (1) fear the unknown (2) test parental response (3) misunderstand
4 - 6	Communicate as if to young adult Reward positive achievement
7 - 9	Appeal to new-found independence Use charts, stars, etc Use fantasy which is enjoyed, though separated from reality
10 - 12	Communicate as if to adult Use praise frequently

This table is included for three reasons:

• A knowledge of psychological/physical development is needed if the dental team is to try to understand a child's reaction to dentistry

• Dental teams cannot view themselves as carers just of the child's teeth.

A more holistic view requires that they also have concern for each child's emotional and physical well-being.

- It will be easier to communicate your concern and interest in a child to the parent if you know the appropriate questions to ask, (e.g. parents are unlikely to be impressed when you ask if their child is walking if the infant has not yet mastered the art of sitting up!)

In addition to the physical and motor abilities detailed in Table 9.1, other factors will affect the level of communication each child has with the dental team. For example, their cognitive abilities, their emotional development, the relationships they have previously formed with the people around them, and the society in which they live will influence how they perceive and react to new events. However, particularly important is their cognitive development. This can be divided into four main stages.

The first stage is that of SENSORI-MOTOR intelligence and this occurs between birth and the age of 2 years. Primarily this stage represents the infant's increasing recognition that objects around them are separate and different entities from themselves.

The second stage is known as the PREOPERATIONAL PHASE and occurs when the child is between the ages of about 2 to 7/8 years. This is the stage where the child begins to comprehend words and their ability to concentrate increases dramatically. They are trying to make sense of the world. However, their view tends to be somewhat distorted and egocentric. In their eyes, the world seems to extend out from a central being that is 'themselves'.

The third stage is the OPERATIONAL PHASE during which a child sees the world as a much more stable place. They recognise that objects and other people are real and can imagine physical objects and people even when they are not present. Children in this stage have a rather pragmatic 'here and now and nothing else' attitude to life.

The final stage of cognitive development is the formal thinking stage, which happens between the ages of 11 and 15 years. During this stage, children can think in the abstract and can deduce things. They can also cope with imagining events some time in the future, which a younger child is not able to do.

Finally, perhaps the most important factor for the dental team to remember about the child patient is that they have not chosen to be in the surgery. They cannot choose not to return if they don't like you (if their parents do!). While an adult will weigh the costs and benefits of dental treatment, and decide that it is worthwhile, a child cannot project himself into the future in the same way.

Table 9.2

Age (months)

1   Beginning to watch mother's face
    Will notice toy or rattle at 15 cm
    Reflex stepping movements on hard surface

3   Waves arms symmetrically
    Visually alert. Watches own hands.
    Clasps and unclasps hands

6   Can sit up with support and can roll over
    Can support self on extended arms
    Reaches out to grasp small objects

9   Progresses by rolling/squirming
    Can stand if something to hold
    Attempting to crawl

12 Can sit up. Crawls efficiently.
    Walks when supported. Drops toys to watch them fall.
    *Drinks from a cup with assistance

15 Walks
    Understands simple commands

18 Runs (but cannot avoid objects)*
    Can scribble
    Has 6 - 20 recognisable words

24 Runs safely
    Throws a ball

*Refers to himself by name
*Copies adults in play

30 200+ words
Constantly asking: Why? Where? When?
Stuttering in eagerness to communicate

36 Draws, recognises colours
Plays make-believe

48 Listens to, and can tell long stories
Eats with spoon and fork
Dresses and undresses
Washes hands and face

60 Skips, dances
Plans and builds
Protective to younger children and pets

*   Indicates phases of development of particular relevance to the
dental team

For children, a bad experience at the surgery may not affect whether they attend regularly as a child. However, a good experience may ensure that once they achieve independence from their parents, they will be likely to consider dental visiting to be an acceptable habit.

Meeting the kids

Firstly, it is important that a child who has an appointment at the surgery is made to feel as if he alone is the focus of attention. Therefore, if possible, it is a good idea for the receptionist to deal directly with the child, and not with the parent or accompanying adult (take the appointment card from the child, address child by name, rather than addressing the parent, explain that the notes are 'a special book about you' to the child ... and so on). Obviously, the type of conversation and degree of interaction will depend on the age of the child, but the golden rule is that the child is the centre of attention and is treated as the 'prized customer', rather the accompanying adult. Most children find this reversal of the adult and child roles very thrilling and will respond warmly to it. A happy child means a happy and satisfied accompanying adult. This patient centred approach can therefore act as a practice builder, even when the patient is a child who has no choice about which practice to attend.

Parents and accompanying adults

Children will almost invariably attend the dental surgery with an accompanying adult. However, increasingly often the person with the child is not the biological parent, nor even the legal guardian. The dental team need to know the relationship (if any) between the adult and child, not only for purposes of consent and legality, but also in order to enhance communication between the team and the child. It is always worthwhile to ask the child: "Who did you bring with you, today?" in order that embarrassment and difficulties are avoided at the outset. Such a question also focuses attention on the child and helps to set the tone for the rest of the visit.

The waiting area

If possible, it is worthwhile to set aside an area of the waiting room and have it as a play area for smaller children. This will serve a dual purpose as many adults have children and will need to leave their child in the waiting room while they themselves have treatment. The play area should contain as wide and as interesting a selection of toys and reading material as you can afford. Children and parents of children will have less time and energy for becoming anxious if they are occupied. A pile of dusty copies of ten-year-old *Horse and Hound* magazines are of scant interest to most six year olds!

It is not necessary or helpful to decorate the walls of the waiting room with dental health education posters. Little attention will be paid to them, and most people know the content of the messages anyway. You will be promoting health more by having a colourful, exciting, noisy waiting room than by promulgating the tired old 'brush your teeth' message.

Time-keeping

Late running of appointments is stressful for both the patient and the dental team. Good time management is therefore an essential element in any practice that wishes its patients to be relaxed and happy. This is even more important for children. Children's time scales are very different from adults.

Remember how the summer holidays seemed to go on forever when you were small? A year was an absolute eternity. Even a week for a child is a very long time because children live only in the present. Each day is a new adventure that will bring both good and bad experiences. However, the impact of an experience tends to be small, once the incident is in the past. This difference in time scale has obvious practical repercussions for the dental team.

- For a bored child sitting in a waiting room, five minutes can seem like an hour.

- How much of the last visit does the child recall - does she remember any of what was said, agreed, promised?

- Does the toothache a child had last night matter to him now? Was the pain experienced for a little time or a long time? (What is a short time to you may seem like centuries to a child).

Names

Once again the issue of names becomes important. It was suggested earlier in the book that it was courteous to refer to older people (other adults) by their title and surname, rather than their forenames. For children the opposite is true, the first name is the appropriate one for the team to address the child, checking if necessary that this is the name that the child usually goes by - (Rebecca may be known as Becky, Anthony as Tony, etc.) because anything which the team can do to make the child feel at ease will be helpful. It is worthwhile making a written note of a child's nickname, if they have one.

However, just because the patient is a child it is not acceptable to forget to introduce the people whom the child will be with during their visit. The nurse can be particularly helpful in this role. The practice members should decide on a policy regarding names by which they should introduce themselves to children. The aim is to make the practice as similar to a child's usual environment as possible. Therefore, although it might seem terribly chummy and friendly for the dentist to be known by his first name to children, many youngsters are not used to addressing adults by their given name. Indeed, some may have in the past been reprimanded for doing so. It might therefore be better, and the child might find it easier, to know the staff as Mr. So and So or Miss Whatsit.

Each practice will need to decide upon what they feel most comfortable with and what they think their patients would prefer. What is certain is that the courtesy of introducing staff members should never be omitted, even with (especially with) children.

Conversation

At the outset of a conversation with an adult, we engage in social exchanges such as nice day, terrible weather, how are you... These are not of themselves actual topics of interest but simple opening gambits, designed to get the ball rolling. Similarly, when meeting a child for the first time you need to have some sort of opening line. Unfortunately, five-year-olds have little awareness of, let alone interest in, the weather. One must therefore find other social exchanges to begin the conversation with when dealing with small children. It is important that it is the child with whom you have the initial conversation, and not the parent, as this sets the tone of the child being the central focus for the team right at the outset.

It is difficult to make suggestions for conversational gambits with children, as they are so varied in their ages, outlooks and social backgrounds. However, experience suggests that addressing questions to children about themselves almost invariably raises a spark of interest. Therefore, any comment about the child's name (lovely, unusual), height (aren't you tall?), age (goodness, you're just the right size for five!), clothes (what a beautiful dress) will usually get a response.

Christmas and birthdays are of course a blessing to conversation with children. The lists of presents received becomes ever longer and therefore one can almost always find some area of mutual experience ("Oh, I got a computer too"). The dental team should always check children's notes for the birth date. If the birthday was last week (or will occur soon) they will then know about it, and can comment appropriately.

In the surgery

When greeting the patient, try not to tower above the child. This will involve squatting down to introduce yourself and in order to establish eye contact.

The question of whether the parent should accompany the child into the surgery is one that has been under debate for many years. A simple solution is to ask the child, thus giving them control, and encouraging them to trust that their wishes are paramount. If they prefer their parent to be with them, then that is what should happen. Usually, younger children will opt for an accompanying adult and adolescents and teenagers will not.

Alternative choice technique

The technique of offering choices is a very useful one, especially with younger, less cooperative children. For example, instead of saying:

> "Will you sit in this big chair now?"
>> say
> "Do you want to get in the chair from that side, or do you want to come round this side to get on?"

Many children are so surprised at being allowed the apparently 'adult' right of making choices that they readily cooperate, even the ones who had come determined to disobey anyone who seemed to be a figure of authority.

Prior to examining a child, a little more conversation is required. A knowledge of children's comics, TV programmes, popular games and pop stars is very useful, but failing this, a joke is often a good solution and is certainly preferable to silence. Children have bizarre senses of humour, often finding the weakest puns hysterically funny. It is very worthwhile to have a collection of kids' jokes in the team's repertoire. The stock can be replenished by asking each child to tell you a joke. Between the ages of about 6 to 8 years this is very popular, and even the shyest children will often become more confident when reciting something which they 'know' is funny.

If you cannot seem to achieve any response or empathy via conversation, children often respond to hearing about the childhood experiences of the adults around them. Most children roar with laughter and are amazingly interested when told that the therapist, when she was little, fell out of a tree she was climbing, into a bed of stinging nettles and got stung all over. Why children have this interest in other people's younger days and most particularly in their misfortunes is not known, but it is true. It can certainly be very useful in the dental surgery.

Taking notes

With child patients, it is as important to record in the notes the keys to communication as it is to write down the clinical procedures carried out. Each child should feel very special and singular in the dental practice, so they will expect you to remember their teacher's name, their favourite programme, their funny joke. They will not recognise that you have many other matters, let alone many other patients, in your mind. Thus, they may feel hurt and forgotten if they have told you something and you have not remembered it. Children's confidences are very special to them. You will build the relationship between the team and the child much more quickly if you appear to always remember something that they told you at the last visit. Thus, making a record in the notes of some of the key issues of what has been said, will be extremely helpful. It also ensures that rapport can continue to be built even when staff absences or appointment changes mean that different team members are seeing the child.

Examining and treating children

The concept of 'Tell Show-Do' is well established in paediatric dentistry. Its importance cannot be over emphasised and it has proved to be effective time and time again. The basic principle is that nothing, but nothing, is done in the surgery without first telling the child - and this must be done in language which they understand and identify with (see below). After the explanation has been given, the child is shown as far as possible what the procedure will be like and exactly what it will mean. Only at this stage does the procedure commence.

For example:

> "I'm going to put on this special light. It shines like the sun so I'd like you to put on some special sunglasses to stop it from being too bright for your eyes."

> "When the special light is on, the magic chair will tip back, then you are going to open your mouth, as wide as a lion. When you do that the inside of your mouth will light up - just like your fridge at home lights up inside so that you can see what's in it."

> "I will use a little mirror to count your teeth. It's a little tiny round

mirror - the size of a spoon. It's on the end of a stick, so that I can look at your very back teeth."

In these explanations, care has been taken to:

- Use words and imagery which the child understands.

- Give the child a reason why each piece of equipment and each procedure is necessary (i.e. the glasses, the light).

When examining children's teeth, it is often useful to explain that you are going to count their teeth. Counting is something children are very familiar with and feel comfortable with. They rather like to guess how many teeth they have (5 million has been the top estimate so far!)

Modelling

Children will often copy other children or siblings, especially if they see the other child receiving attention and praise. Therefore, a recalcitrant child will often participate in a dental examination if another suitable, confident child is available to set an example and be suitably rewarded for doing so.

Failing the presence of other children, it is sometimes useful, with younger patients, to have toys in the surgery that can be used to 'model' behaviour.

For example:
"You look at Teddy's mouth with this little mirror, then I'll look at yours."

In fact, toys and glove puppets with teeth have been specifically designed with this type of use in mind. However, our experience suggests that it is the team's behaviour rather than how realistic the toy is, which influences the patient's reactions.

Words

The words used during a child's treatment are very important. Children are very influenced by past associations with words. Therefore positive framing of each explanation can make a phenomenal difference to a visit. Similarly, using images that the child likes, and is familiar with, can dramatically increase the amount of treatment they will accept.

For example, when describing the action of the handpiece, you can tell the child that it will tickle their finger when you run the burr on their nail. You will find that they almost invariably laugh when the burr comes into contact with the finger. The word 'tickle' is so associated in the child's mind with a pleasurable amusing sensation that using the word seems to, on its own, induce that sensation (classical conditioning). Thus, if a child, having had the handpiece demonstrated to them, is told that you are going to "tickle the naughty germs out of the tooth" and to "listen for the germs laughing" - they will find the whole procedure funny, and very often laugh out loud at the thought of tickled germs laughing.

Taking care to use the best word possible makes a great deal of difference to children's cooperation, although it does require that the team put their own egos and embarrassments to one side and concentrate solely and utterly on making the child happy. The team need to be imaginative, and supportive of each other's tomfoolery. Idiotic some of this may seem, but experience shows that it works.

Item	Example of Possible Description to Child
Polishing brush	Electric toothbrush
Round head burr	Machine to tickle the bad germs out of the tooth
Amalgam	Silver star pushed into tooth to stop more germs getting in
Caries	Germs in wellingtons with sticky soles (The Sticky Wellie Germs!)
Fissure sealant	Magic sticky paint which will catch the SWGs
Dental chair	Special rocket man's chair
Relative analgesia	Magic wind
Aspirator	Straw for nurse to suck the water away
Compressed air dryer	Tiny hairdryer
Water jet	Water pistol (Take care, you may end up very wet!)

The 'difficult' child

Imagine a pleasant, well behaved child comes to your practice. It is likely that the dental team will respond favourably, will like the child and will therefore want to do their very best for him. Given that children tend to live up or down to the expectations others have of them, in such an environment the child will react favourably, this in turn will endear the child to the team even further.

If the team is faced with a badly behaved, rude child, the dislike and negative vibes that this arouses will be likely to reduce cooperation even further.

The general aim for the team is to encourage 'good' behaviour by offering positive reinforcement when it occurs. However, this can be a problem. A child who behaves well tends to be ignored because everyone concentrates on the procedure with the intention of completing it as quickly as possible.

Children who make a fuss will receive attention. The procedure may even stop and he may be consoled by the parent. If you view this in terms of operant conditioning (Chapter 5) it is clear that the dental team tends to punish 'good' behaviours (child sits still and the discomfort continues while child is ignored) and rewards 'bad' behaviours (non-acceptance of treatment results in attention and the stopping of the procedure). Whilst no one would nowadays suggest that a crying objecting child should be physically forced to undergo treatment, the team must guard against 'rewarding' behaviour that is not conducive to health. Constant attention, support, praise and reinforcement should be given to children when they cope well with treatment. They do not know you are pleased and impressed unless you tell them so. Even more importantly, if a child has done well (e.g. improved their oral hygiene, coped well with a filling for the first time) make sure that you praise the child to the parent. This acts as a very powerful reward to most children.

Closing remarks

The principal emotion children experience when they meet a new situation is fear. Fear is a very natural reaction, which developed in order that we could survive. A child visiting a dental practice has two possible reasons to be fearful. One is fear of the unknown. The child is facing a set of circumstances which he may not have encountered before or does not remember. Or they may be uncertain whether their experience at the last visit will be the same as at this one. The child, in essence, does not know what will happen to him. How he reacts to this will depend on previous life experiences. If the home and school life has been largely pleasant, predictable and adults have consistently acted as trustworthy beings, the child will assume (unless he has been fed 'horror' stories about dentistry) that life will continue to be so even within dental practice walls. He may therefore treat a dental visit with stoicism or even enjoyment. It is vital, in such a case, that this trust is not destroyed by misleading or frightening the child by doing anything unexpected.

Other children may unfortunately have had life experiences that have suggested to them that new situations can lead to unpleasant occurrences. They are therefore bound to be worried and scared when faced by an unknown set of people in a strange environment.

Many writers have attempted to document 'management' techniques for children. It is the authors' view that there is no universal panacea, no formulae, for dealing with children, because each one is an individual. Thus, the keys to dealing successfully with them are, in general, listening and mentally noting all the verbal and non-verbal communications, and empathetic handling. However, each member of the team will need to invent their own techniques for dealing with a given child in a given situation. The Tell-Show-Do principle is helpful, but the words used when telling should be not only comprehensive but meaningful to the child. That is: the explanations should try, as far as possible, to recreate images and situations that the child recognises from the day-to-day world he inhabits.

Thus, each member of the dental team will have to cast their mind back and try to remember what it felt like to be a child. If possible, they should allow themselves to re-inhabit that world and be a child. Imagination and playfulness can assist communication with almost any child.

In general however, the best tool for dealing with children, especially those ones who we label as 'difficult' is a genuine affection for all of them, however they behave and whatever their oral health status.

Further reading

Fayle SA, Tahmassebi JF. Paediatric dentistry in the new millennium: 2. Behaviour management-helping children to accept dentistry. *Dent Update* 2003 **30**: 294-298.

Folayan MO, Idehen F. Factors influencing the use of behavioral management techniques during child management by dentists. *J Clin Pediatr Dent* 2004 **28**:155-161.

Other 'Special' Patients

10

"Enlarge the opportunity and the person will expand to fill it".

Many dental teams view with some degree of dread, visits from the very elderly, the mentally handicapped, and those who have severe medical problems. This chapter is included in order that the dental team may view such patients with stoicism, even though the visit requires particular effort and a high degree of communication skills from them. The individuals in these categories are as much a part of the community as the fit, well and communicative patient and thus are as, if not more, deserving of the team's special attentions.

The older patients

The proportion of elderly people within the population is rising steadily, it is therefore likely that communication with, and care for, this group will become an increasingly important component of a modern general dental practice. Therefore, it is necessary that each member of the dental team has an interest in, and empathy with, older people. This section is included because, although most of us feel well-disposed towards older and elderly people, unlike with children, most of us do not have our own experiences to draw upon when seeking to understand them. The aim here is to attempt to clear up some of the misconceptions about ageing, in order that dental teams are able to respond to the problems of this group in appropriate and effective ways. Your team may have the very best of intentions, but will be unable to help an old person if they are unable to communicate well and get on to the same 'wavelength'.

There is an inevitable tendency for dental teams to slip into jargon. Indeed it is easy, when working all day with other dental professionals who speak the same language, to forget that 'gingivitis', 'caries', 'amalgams' are not everyday words. With elderly people, it is vital that opaque technical terms are avoided, but at the same time it is important that we do not assume that just because someone is old and perhaps a little deaf, they are ignorant. To do so places us in danger of slipping into patronising language. It is vital that we remember that although an older person may have some physical and/or mental problems, they should still be regarded as responsible adults and not as naughty, rather simple-minded children.

What's in a name?

The patronising attitude, which is all too commonly adopted by professionals when dealing with frail elderly people, tends to be reflected in the way we address them. Imagine you were a well-educated, elderly person from a somewhat privileged background. Having been treated with respect by fellow professionals and neighbours all your life and, having been addressed for 60 years as 'Miss So-and-So', imagine how you would feel (even if you were unable to clearly communicate your feelings) when a 17-year-old dental nurse addresses you as 'Betty'. Worse perhaps, would be if she patronises you with pet names such as 'dear', or 'love'. It is terribly easy to forget that the elderly people, with whom we might deal, have usually held down responsible jobs, raised families, owned houses, fought in wars, etc. They have an expectation to be treated with due respect and this expectation should be honoured.

Can you hear me?

As age increases, hearing decreases, but the rate at which this occurs is highly variable. However, the deafness associated with ageing is known as presbycusis, and understanding the characteristics of this type of deafness may assist the team's ability to communicate well with their older patients.

In a patient suffering from early presbycusis the parts of speech that they fail to hear are high-pitched sounds. Unfortunately, consonants are high-pitched sounds and vowels low-pitched. Therefore an elderly person tends to hear only the vowel parts of speech.

Thus:

>"Do you brush your denture each night?"
>> becomes
>"Oo oo uh oo e uuh ee i"

Articulating your consonants particularly clearly may help elderly people to understand what you are saying.

Presbycusis has another feature that it is important for the dental team to keep in mind. The elderly person may find it difficult to hear soft sounds but loud sounds become distorted and amplified, with the effect that the words cannot be distinguished. This paradox explains why someone who has been asking you to repeat everything because they cannot hear you may become annoyed and say: "no need to shout, I'm not deaf" when you raise your voice in an attempt to communicate.

A further difficulty, which the elderly person may experience, is an inability to separate the conversation in which they are involved from surrounding noises and chatter. Thus, ensuring that the environment around the conversation is as quiet as possible will go a long way to enhancing effective communication.

And, as with communication with anyone, a large part of the message is conveyed, not by words but by the accompanying facial gestures and body language (Chapter 3), so providing a well-lit room and appropriate seating positions will help.

When talking to elderly people with hearing problems the keys are:

- Accentuate consonants
- Speak clearly but do not shout
- Moderate the pace of your speech
- Ensure a quiet environment
- Accompany words with appropriate gestures and facial expressions.

The first chapter highlighted that one of the essential components of effective communication in the surgery is appreciation of the patient's problems. Deafness is as frustrating for the 'listener' as it is to the speaker. If both parties appreciate the difficulties and act together in an attempt to make progress with the patient's oral health, much can be achieved.

What did you say?

It is worthwhile noting here that some older people may have speech difficulties. Dysphasia is a condition in which the person speaking articulates inappropriate words, but is completely unaware that they are talking in a way that is meaningless. In their own mind they are communicating perfectly well. Such people can become extremely frustrated when the listener does not respond appropriately to what they think they have said. Communication with dysphasic people is difficult in the extreme, and the attention of a speech therapist should be sought, if this has not already been done. The dental team need to be aware of this condition and if they encounter a person with this problem, must avoid labelling them as 'dotty' and try to remember that an alert and sane person is trying to tell them something. Remembering this and trying to understand the anger and frustration that the person must feel will perhaps prevent the team from assuming simply that the elderly person is uncooperative and aggressive.

A further communication problem which elderly people may suffer from, which is quite separate from dysphasia (see above), is dysarthria. In dysarthria, the nerves and muscles required for clear speech are damaged, resulting in slurred and unintelligible speech. This is particularly important to the dental team as similar problems may result from poorly fitting dentures. Much can be done to improve the quality of life for elderly people, simply by ensuring that they have the best possible denture, in terms of their appearance, speech and ability to chew.

Dementia

Dementia is due to organic changes in a person's brain, which result in mental impairment. Whilst the dental team need to recognise that the information given by such patients may be unreliable, it is also important not to assume that there is no point in talking to them. The social contact brought about by a trip to a dental practice can bring a great source of enjoyment to an elderly, demented person.

Apathy

It is sometimes the case that elderly people become withdrawn and unresponsive. This may be indicative of depression, but equally may simply be due to social isolation. Being alone for much of the day causes people to get out of the habit of engaging in conversation. Again, the practice may be a bright spot in an old person's life, even though he may be unable to communicate. Even with the most apathetic and uncommunicative old people, it is important that the dental team avoid talking over the patient as if they were not a sentient being. People are people, not objects, no matter their degree of handicap.

The patient with learning difficulties

It is not possible in a text of this nature to offer advice on communication with patients with learning difficulties as if they were a homogenous group of people, all with the same needs and requirements. In general, a person is described as having learning difficulties if there is delay in reaching, or failure to reach, the various stages of development described in Chapter 9. Usually, the delay has to be consistent and is demonstrated by a delay of a third or more of the age at which the milestones are normally achieved, e.g. if the child cannot walk by the age of 2 years, or say a short sentence by the age of 3 years. There are hundreds of causes of learning difficulties and infinite variation in the abilities and behaviours of people with them. Learning difficulties can vary from the most severe disability, in which the person's existence is merely vegetative, to people in who there are few outward signs of any impairment.

Thus, it is sufficient to say that communication with someone who has some form of learning difficulty should proceed much as for any other patient, i.e. the person should be treated at all times as an individual, with preferences, needs and desires which are unique to them.

As the relationship between the dental team and the patient develops, the team will learn the limits of the person's comprehension and understanding and at this point will adjust their communication accordingly. Many people with learning difficulties are capable of much more than you might, on first meeting, expect. It is therefore vital that the team tries not to stereotype, judge or classify the patient but explores in full how they may best help the person concerned.

Suffice to say that in our experience, very rewarding relationships can be built with people whose intellectual capacity is substantially less than 'normal'. In addition, especially amongst those who are institutionalised, the dental surgery may become one of the places where the mentally impaired person is treated as an individual in their own right and gets half an hour or so of another person's individual attention. Quite remarkable degrees of cooperation and oral health can, with patience, be achieved. Just as for other patients, the team need to try to work out exactly what is important to the individual concerned and must attempt to relate to those needs, rather than the goal of perfect clinical dentistry.

Medically disabled patients

The term 'medically disabled' refers to patients who are suffering from some type of chronic illness, such that physical or social functioning is limited in some way. Many texts are available which detail the relationship of the myriad illnesses in this category with oral problems. The aim of this section is not to reiterate the details of 'oral medicine' but to touch lightly on how the presence of medical disability may affect communication within the dental surgery.

Why are you asking me?

Because of the relationship alluded to above (between medical conditions, drug regimes and oral health) and because a full medical history must be taken by the dental team in order to fulfil medico-legal requirements, it is neither possible nor desirable to avoid discussing patients' medical problems with them. However, on occasions, the dental team may find that patients are unwilling to disclose medical details. Some patients may regard their medical history as a personal matter that should only be discussed between themselves and their medical practitioner. Such people may exhibit a degree of antipathy towards members of the team who ask probing questions about their medical history. This is usually due to one of the four reasons listed below, all of which can be easily dealt with by using a careful approach and sensitivity to the person's views.

- The patient may not understand why their medical history is of any relevance to the dental team.

- Patients may not wish to be regarded as exceptional in any way, especially if they suspect that their condition may limit the dental treatment options available to them.

- If patients' medical conditions involve personal or intimate difficulties, they may not wish to reveal the illness to someone whom they regard as a relative stranger.

- Some patients become so used to their 'medically compromised' state that they fail to mention it. This is because they do not regard themselves as being 'abnormal' in any way.

Most of these barriers to communication will be overcome by a careful explanation as to why a medical history is being taken, i.e. because oral problems may result from some medical conditions, because medical conditions can affect which treatment /medicines are 'best' for the patient and because some medicines taken for other reasons can react to produce oral symptoms/drug interactions.

It will be necessary to undertake this explanation in a sensitive manner, as some medically compromised patients may feel somehow 'discriminated' against as a result of their condition (e.g. epileptics, HIV+ patients) and it is therefore important to react to revelations of such conditions in a non-judgemental fashion. Again, careful explanation of the relationship between the dental team's function (maximising oral health) and the patient's medical status will go some way to reassuring the patient that the dental team is acting in their best interests.

If the patient's responses to medical history taking reveal a problem of an intimate or potentially embarrassing nature (bowel problems, sexually transmitted diseases), extreme sensitivity during questioning is required. Careful observation of the patient's non-verbal communication should adequately demonstrate the patient's feelings about their 'illness' to the dental team. Determining the patient's reaction to their own problems will dictate the best 'tone' in which to pursue the questions that need to be asked. For some, this will be a strictly 'professional, no-nonsense' attitude, while for others, empathetic reactions to small pieces of information will ensure that the full history is revealed.

Finally, some patients will have completely normalised their illness. Well-controlled diabetics often exemplify this type of reaction to being questioned about a medically compromising condition. A patient who is managing their medical condition in a way which means that it has no impact whatever on their social and physical functioning may actually forget that their 'illness' has any meaning to anyone other than themselves, and even then only in terms of management. It is therefore important to ask direct questions about diabetes, epilepsy, etc. as patients can omit to mention these conditions, not because they feel that they have anything to hide, or because they are being dishonest, but simply because when asked if there is anything 'wrong' with them, their truthful answer is "no".

Patients with incurable and fatal conditions

On occasion, the dental team may have to deal with patients who are suffering from a terminal illness. The way in which such patients are dealt with will, once again, depend on the individual and their response to their particular condition and approaching death. Some terminally ill people welcome the opportunity to relate to new people, but do not wish to discuss their condition in anything but the most cursory way. Others will wish to share their problems with members of the team. We would favour an approach to such patients in which listening is more important than providing information and treatment. Of course, any treatment which enhances the quality of the person's remaining life should be instituted, but only if the patient (not the dental team) believes it to be worthwhile. When talking to people who are coming to terms with, or have already come to terms with, the prospect of dying, it often emerges that the patient's main fears are the process of dying, or its effect on others, rather than fear of death itself.

There may also be terminally ill patients who are referred to the dentist for treatment by the patient's physician. In this case, it is wise to consult with the medical practitioner prior to seeing the patient, in order that the dental team can be made aware of the precise nature and probable course of the patient's illness. It will also be necessary to find out whether or not the patient is aware of the severity and prognosis of his disease. Many such patients, even if they have not been told directly, will actually have guessed what is likely to happen to them. In such cases, care must be taken not to tell patients facts that have hitherto remained unmentioned, if not unknown. Patients who really do not wish to be faced with dealing with a terminal disease are remarkably adept at shutting themselves off from it. This 'denial' is a psychological defence mechanism and is very effective. The dental team should have no role in attempting to break this down and must therefore attempt to deal with the patient as the patient wishes to be dealt with.

The HIV positive patient

It is increasingly likely that most dental teams will have to deal with patients who are known to be HIV positive, on a routine basis. Much has been written about the oral health of HIV positive individuals and AIDS patients, yet few texts offer advice on relevant aspects of communication.

Here it must be reiterated that all patients could be HIV positive. The dental team who deems that it can identify 'high-risk' individuals by their demeanour, etc. is taking stereotyping (Chapter 3) to an extreme, and the erroneous belief that homosexual men, and intravenous drug users can be 'spotted' should be emphatically discouraged. Medical history taking should be the same for all patients. People who know that they are HIV positive will have made decisions about revealing their status before entering the surgery, and therefore probing questioning of those whom you have convinced yourself are 'at-risk' will only serve to alienate patients, particularly those whom you have wrongly assigned to this category.

Dental teams who treat HIV positive patients will be dealing with patients who are well, but whose life expectancy might be diminished. They are also treating patients who are aware of their own potential infectivity. Again, since the patient has thrown them self open to possible discrimination in order to help the team protect themselves, it seems only courteous they are treated with appropriate respect and civility. Remember, it would be much easier for such patients to lie by omission and fail to disclose their positive status.

Patients who are HIV positive may have already faced rejection from sexual partners and a degree of social rejection. They will therefore be likely to greatly appreciate recognition of their status and empathy about the implications of the condition. Also, explanation about the importance of scrupulous oral hygiene, and description of signs and symptoms to watch for, may well be very important to them. It offers them some degree of control, even though it is only over a small part of their health. This can be very life-enhancing.

Last thoughts

If this chapter was to encompass every type of patient who might pose unusual communication challenges to the dental team, it would comprise a list of every single individual who might attend a dental practice. Every person brings with them their own personality and personal difficulties. Treating elderly, disabled and ill patients sometimes requires that the dental team stretch their ability to 'put themselves in the other person's shoes' to its absolute limit. Vast amounts have been written about the physical, technical and medical skills of treating 'special' patients. However, you will find that dealing with real patients, in real situations, is often more complex than such texts reveal, because of the personalities of the patients involved. It is very difficult to define a particular 'way' of 'managing' a particular 'sort' of patient. Because there are no absolutes, the views expressed in this chapter are those of the authors. If the reader disagrees with the points raised, that can only be for the good, because the reader will then address the issues and make decisions about the problems for themselves.

Further reading

DePaola G. Managing the care of patients infected with bloodborne diseases. *J Am Dent Assoc* 2003 **134**: 350-358.

Gratten MA, Vasques AE. Age related hearing loss: current research. *Curr Opin Otolaryngol Head Neck Surg* 2003 **11**: 367-371.

Nordenram G, Ronnberg L, Winblad B. The perceived importance of appearance and oral function, comfort and health for severely demented persons rated by relatives, nursing staff and hospital dentists. *Gerodontology* 1994 **11**:18-24.

Shapiro J, Mosqueda L, Botros D. A caring partnership: expectations of ageing persons with disabilities for their primary care doctors. *Fam Pract* 2003 **20**: 635-641.

Decisions in Dentistry: Whose Responsibility?

"Whenever you accept our views we shall be in full agreement with you"

Moshe Dayan
(during Arab-Israeli negotiations 1977)

11

Introduction

The idea of shared responsibility for a patient's health, with the major onus being on the patient rather than the professional, may be regarded as rather strange. There is a view (somewhat prevalent among dental teams), which suggests that there is no need for a patient to share the responsibility either for their mouth, or for them to become involved in treatment decisions. Instead, patients are often simply expected to comply with the suggestions that the professional makes and consent to treatment because of their faith in the dental team.

This idea that because we are 'experts', people should defer to our decisions, and treat us in the respectful manner which is traditional, seems at the very least old fashioned, and at worst, arrogant in the extreme. People who are experts in other fields have to communicate their specialist knowledge to each and every individual, in a way that can be easily understood, even by people who do not have the same expertise. For example, although an accountant would not expect you to understand tax law, you would be dismayed if he could not communicate the principles underlying what needed to be done in order to reduce your tax bill. In fact, in most fields someone would not be regarded as an 'expert' or as someone with specialist knowledge unless they were able to share their expert assessments of a situation. Consider teachers and pupils. Pupils may defer to teachers simply because they are teachers, but they cannot learn through such a relationship. If teachers took the attitude that they do not have to explain matters, or that children will accrue understanding simply because the teacher knows best, where would we be?

There is simply no good reason why conversations between dentists and patients should not 'translate' specialist knowledge, so that all parties can participate in decision making and treatment planning. It is not possible to either offer patients the best care available or to make rational treatment plans unless a true dialogue is taking place.

This chapter aims to describe the importance of, and difficulties involved in, communication relating to clinical decisions.

Quality care

The following section is based on the assumption that the objective of clinical dental care is to offer the best possible solution for a given problem for each **individual** patient.

> Quality care is offered when you choose a course of action which will:
>
> Increase the probability of an outcome the patient regards as 'good' and at the same time
> Decrease the probability of an outcome the patient regards as 'poor'

This definition of quality care moves us away from the idea that if there is disease it must be treated in a particular way. For example, if a patient presents with a decayed and painful tooth, in some instances extracting the tooth will be the best option. Choosing to take the tooth out will relieve the patient's pain. It will also ensure that the tooth will never give the patient further trouble. Alternatively, the tooth could be restored. This second option may offer the patient relief from pain, but there is still a possibility of further toothache, and the restoration will almost certainly have to be replaced at some time in the future. Thus, the clinician has to weigh the small risk of further trouble from a restored tooth, against the problems of losing a tooth that may then need to be replaced with a denture. Which of the options represents the best solution? Well, this will depend on the value the patient puts on each of the possible outcomes. That evaluation in turn will depend on the attitudes, beliefs and lifestyle of the person involved. Therefore, a dentist cannot possibly make a sensible comparison of how 'good' each outcome from treatment will be, unless he can communicate well with the patient. Returning to the extraction/restoration problem, the best solution will be dependent upon just how much the patient wishes to retain the tooth, their attitude to their mouth and appearance, and their views about restorative care. Therefore, their preferences and choices will to some extent depend upon their past experiences of dentistry.

A dental professional's ability to offer good quality care therefore depends partly, but not solely on personal dental expertise and knowledge. A dentist must be able to assess how likely or unlikely various outcomes are, whenever a treatment decision is made. However, quality care is also dependent on the dental team's communication skills, in that they must be able to determine how valuable (or distressing or inconvenient) the patient thinks both the processes and the outcomes of dental treatment will be.

Every time a decision is made in the dental surgery, we should have decided:

- Have I considered all the possible solutions to this problem?

- What chance events might affect the outcome? (e.g. teeth sometimes break during extraction)

- Taking into account all possible solutions and all possible chance events, what outcomes can we potentially end up with?

- How likely, or unlikely, are the chance events?
  (A dentist who undertakes many extractions will know what proportion end up with surgical extractions)

- Of all of the things that could happen as a result of this decision, which outcome would the patient value most highly?

It is important when enumerating treatment options for a given case, to always consider the option of doing nothing. Quite often this might lead to a good outcome, a primary tooth might exfoliate naturally, thus avoiding the unpleasantness of an extraction. At the very least, doing nothing may lead to an outcome which is no worse than the status quo. Leaving a tooth unfilled for six months, even in the presence of decay will, in a regular attender, lead to a filled tooth later rather than sooner - the only difference in the outcome, if you choose to leave the decayed tooth alone, is the time at which this outcome is achieved.

Finally, it is important when enumerating treatment options to consider the things which might go wrong, to imagine the results if the treatment fails. Too often, dental professionals take particular decisions because they have forgotten what the consequences of failure might be. Talented dental professionals are aware of risks and have contingency plans for action in the event of untoward outcomes from treatment.

How valuable are teeth?

Making good clinical decisions requires good communication skills and an ability to see the process of care, and the outcomes of treatment, through the patient's eyes. Remember, what dentists consider to be a 'good' outcome, may not be the same as what the patient thinks. The value the patient places on treatment outcomes is infinitely more important (in terms of health care and patient satisfaction) than achieving what is, in the dentist's view, a perfect clinical result.

For example, a dentist may consider that three or four visits in order to achieve a perfectly root filled tooth is perfectly acceptable. However, think back to the Health Belief Model (Chapter 2). The benefits of treatment are only valuable and worthwhile to the patient if the benefits outweigh the costs. In the case of the three-visit root treatment, to the patient the saving of a tooth just may not be worth the discomfort, cost and time off work which would be involved. The value that a patient places on an outcome should always be of paramount importance and is the basis of good clinical decision making. It is that value (the patient's) which determines what is 'good' or 'bad' about an outcome, NOT the dental team's views about their handiwork.

A 'good' clinical decision raises the probability of reaching outcomes, which to the patient have high value, whilst concomitantly lowering the probability of events which (in the patient's eyes) have low value. Thus, no matter how skilled the clinician is in terms of knowledge and technique, it is the ability to elicit from a patient the attitudes upon which outcome evaluation depends, which is the mark of a truly skilled practitioner. Treatment, or withholding it, cannot ever be justified simply on the basis of the amount of pathology. What constitutes the best treatment for each patient is dictated by what outcome can be achieved, and how valuable this is to the patient.

Dentistry is about health care for individuals, not about the treatment of pathology in mouths.

Informed choice for patients

Patients cannot participate in choices about their health unless they are given the requisite information in an understandable form. Therefore, the clinician must use his professional expertise, experience and knowledge in order to assess the risks and probabilities involved in each treatment option (including doing nothing) and must then communicate these to the patient. This may sound simple but is in fact quite difficult to do. Instead of simply telling a patient what you are going to do, you might consider offering patients options by using phrases such as:

"There is an 80% chance that I can save the tooth."

However, does this sound the same to a patient as saying:

"One out of five teeth having this treatment will need to be extracted."

Does the meaning of the phrase change if you say:

"Only one out of five teeth having this treatment need to be extracted?"

The simple addition of the word 'only' might dramatically alter the patient's perception of the situation. Also, the way in which the possible consequences are framed might change the patient's understanding. In the example above, you might use a positive 'frame', such as:

"80% of the teeth which have this treatment go on to be healthy"

rather than using the word 'save' (a word which is connected to deeds of heroism). Similarly, information given in terms of percentage success, or percentage failure, also alters how the patient views the information given.

You might think that the easiest solution to this dilemma is to simply decide what you think is best, and go ahead. But to do so is to assume that you are more able to attach a value to dental health outcomes than the patient. This cannot possibly be so, since your life and what you think important may be completely different from that of the patient.

So, if offering numerical probabilities only serves to confuse patients, what about using phrases to convey the chance of something occurring instead? Phrases such as 'poor chance', 'doubtful', 'reasonable to assume' are often used in consultations. But what does a patient understand by such terms?

It is difficult to know, as each individual will react differently.

There is no simple solution to the difficulty of conveying risks and probabilities to patients. However, what is certain, is that the clinician must make a very careful assessment as to how best to convey such information to a given individual and must attempt to ascertain that whatever has been said has been fully understood. It is known that a patient's risk-acceptance is an essential component of their satisfaction with treatment (especially if the treatment does not go according to plan). Good clinical decisions simply cannot be made unless the clinician knows the probability of outcomes, has conveyed these to the patient, and has recognised how the patient views the risks involved. It is also true that unless this is done, a patient cannot truly be said to have given informed consent to the treatment.

The above details how important it is to be able to accurately predict the probability of the events that might occur subsequent to dental treatment. This ability comes from our training and our knowledge of pathology, physiology, anatomy, pharmacology, epidemiology, etc. However, knowing this information is insufficient: the dental team must also be able to communicate the information to the patient if the patient is to truly participate in clinical decisions and really be offered quality care. Lastly, a third and vital piece of information is required if the best treatment decisions are going to be made. We need to know how valuable the outcomes of treatment are to a given patient. For example, for some people the obvious solution to an aching tooth is to have it removed, whilst for others, the loss of a tooth would seem like a hideous and tragic event.

Defining the problem

The very first stage in the planning of dental treatment is, as detailed in Chapter 1, defining exactly what that patient's problem (not disease status) is. In order to do this, the dental team must talk to the patient, find out what reason the patient gives for attending the surgery, and determine the significance of the problem, and the patient's feelings about dental treatment. The team also needs at this stage to decide what must be done to address the patient's problem and what could be done to enhance the patient's health and well-being. For example, for a patient with severe toothache, the dentist might decide to remove a tooth in order to relieve the pain, and then improve the patient's appearance by fitting a bridge. It is very important that the difference between that which is necessary in order to achieve the patient's current objectives (relief of pain), and the treatments that are advisable/possible in order to achieve dental health objectives (a functioning dentition), are carefully explained to the patient. Otherwise, patients may see the treatment as a 'package' and believe that they require it all in order to address their problem. If this is the case, we are removing patient choice.

Gather information

The second stage in treatment planning is gathering and analysing all the facts that might be relevant to the treatment decision making process. This might include the patient's social history, the amount of time and money the patient is able, or prepared, to spend on their mouth, and, importantly the effort in home care which the patient is prepared to make. It is important to keep in mind, when planning treatment, that embarking on treatments that subsequently require monumental efforts on the patient's part in order to maintain the results, will lead to poor outcomes if these efforts are beyond the patient's capabilities.

Enumerate options

The dental professional must, once in possession of all the relevant facts, consider all the possible options that might lead to a resolution of the patient's problem. It is important that all possibilities are presented to the patient in a meaningful unbiased way in order for them to be able to make an informed choice and make their values and preferences clear to the carer. If the dentist only offers the first feasible solution that comes to mind, then the patient will be forced to choose that course of action. If other options are not explored, the best solution will be in danger of being overlooked. The best solution to a problem is not always the most obvious one.

Evaluate options

If a number of possible solutions rather than just one were identified and discussed together, the clinician and the patient must decide which solution gives an outcome that the patient prefers. For example, an aching tooth can be extracted. This offers the patient:

- A certain end to their pain
- A guarantee of no further problems from the tooth
- Cheap treatment
- A potentially aesthetically displeasing appearance.

Or, the tooth might be root treated, which offers the patient:

- Potential further discomfort
- Several dental visits
- A retained tooth.

Thus, the problem (the pain) is solved by either solution but both the process and the end outcomes are very different.

Last thoughts

It is very easy, when acting as a health care professional, especially one who is revered for their expertise, to slip into a somewhat paternalistic role. In the past, patients have merely been informed of what treatment they 'should' have. It is being increasingly recognised that both the relationship between dental profession and patient, and patient satisfaction are improved by mutual participation in choices about oral health and dental care. To achieve this mutually acceptable dialogue requires immense effort on the part of the dental team, and the clinician needs to know the true probability of success for each type of treatment. This information needs to be passed on to the patient, as informed choices are impossible without this process.

It is no longer acceptable not to be aware of the consumer voice in health care. We cannot continue to think of disease as a simple disruption of the normal workings of the body's anatomy or physiology. Patients and their body parts are not like machines that 'break down' and thus need to be repaired. Health is a feeling of well-being and control, not just the absence of pathology. The roles of 'the sick' and 'the healer' are no longer appropriate. If we are to truly provide what our patients need (rather than what we think they need) and provide real quality care, the decisions we make in the dental surgery must take account of the individual's functional, psychological and social well-being, as well as their disease status.

If ever we find ourselves slipping into an: 'I know best, so that's what they're getting' attitude to our patients, it is useful to reflect for a moment, "Whose teeth are they anyway? Yours, or the patient's?"

Further reading

Kay EJ, Nuttall NM. *Clinical Decision Making.* London: British Dental Journal, 1996.

Case Histories- Test the Team

12

"Life can only be understood backwards but it must be viewed forwards".

Soren Kierkegaard

This chapter comprises descriptions of four people, known to the authors. The aim of including these case histories is to allow the reader to test whether or not the information in this book has been of use to them. Each of the people described here actually exist, and each has presented particular problems, difficulties and challenges to dental teams. These case histories are best used as discussion points for dental teams, perhaps at a practice meeting. The cases are chosen to demonstrate how the team can: deal with 'difficult' patients, negotiate treatment planning with patients, decide upon policy about ethical problems, use communication skills in order to market their practice and use personal information about patients to direct clinical care.

These cases will not allow teams to truly exercise their skills with communication and negotiation, since they cannot actually converse and interact with the individuals described in the chapter, but it is hoped that there is sufficient information to allow the cases to act as talking points. There are no 'right' or 'wrong' answers for these patients, but descriptions are provided of how the people were dealt with and what difficulties were encountered. This has been done for interest and with the intention of promoting further discussion.

Case One

Sandra is a 29-year-old single mother. Her daughter is 5-years-old. She lives on income support, but supplements this income by singing in nightclubs. She has a partial acrylic denture replacing her upper left central and lateral incisors. She informs you that the natural teeth were lost during the course of domestic violence with a man whom she no longer sees.

She strikes you as a peculiarly aggressive person.

Sandra claims to be 'phobic' of dentistry and says she cannot bear for any treatment to be carried out, except under general anaesthesia. She blames this phobia on an extraction that took place when a tooth was not properly anaesthetised, during which she fled from the dentist's surgery halfway through the procedure.

On questioning, Sandra revealed that she had been advised to attend your surgery by a friend. She also admitted that she had made several attempts to telephone, but had cut the call off when the 'phone was answered. It is clear from what Sandra says that it was only the receptionist's welcoming tones that made it possible for Sandra to go through with the ordeal of making the appointment. Much of this information was gleaned in the course of casual conversation with the dental nurse and not with the dentist. Sandra's responses to questions from the dentist (despite the dentist's considerable interpersonal skills) were largely monosyllabic, and/or aggressive. This was perhaps understandable as her trust in dentists, particularly male ones, was apparently zero.

Sandra wishes you to 'sort her teeth out' and seems unwilling to participate in any discussion about how this might be achieved.

On examination under relative analgesia, you note draining sinuses related to the heavily restored upper right central and lateral incisors, fair oral hygiene, with no evidence of periodontal involvement. The posterior teeth are heavily restored, but in reasonable condition.

How are you going to proceed with this patient?

Consider particularly:

- How Sandra came to arrive at your surgery
- The objectives of treatment
- What the key motivators for oral health are for the patient
- The patient's 'health locus of control' (See Chapter 5)
- What do you say to the patient after the first visit?
- Who might be the most appropriate people to talk to Sandra?

Case Two

Helen is a 27-year-old single girl. She is highly fashion conscious, was educated at Cheltenham Ladies College and then became a 'hippie' for four years. She now owns and runs a riding school and therefore works outdoors. She is underweight, smokes at least 30 cigarettes per day and a diet analysis reveals that she consumes at least 10 cups of tea every day, each with at least two spoonfuls of sugar. She also claims that she only has time to eat a 'proper meal' two or three times a week. During a working day she eats three to four chocolate bars, several other 'sweets' and consumes two to three cans of sweetened carbonated drinks, which she says she needs to give her 'energy'. She wishes you to place a 'gold tooth' in a gap that is visible when she smiles, which is due to the loss of an upper left first premolar.

Helen has no fear of treatment and claims to brush and floss her teeth daily.

On examination you find that all her remaining posterior teeth are heavily restored, with all the first permanent molars having been extracted and the upper right first premolar and second molar being badly broken down, but symptom-free. The upper left second molar has evidence of secondary caries and there are periodontal pockets of up to 4mm on several teeth. Her oral hygiene appears to be good.

In conversation with Helen, it became clear that she was very much a here-and-now person, with little concern for the future. She was quite fascinatingly unconcerned about her health. For example, when her smoking habit was discussed, her response was: "Well, you can't see my lungs". When shown her decayed teeth, she was quite happy for any work that was required to be done, but seemed to view the issue of changing her diet as somewhat ridiculous. She liked the food she ate, she wasn't overweight, and any damage done to her teeth could be 'fixed', so why change? This is a classic example of someone with a high sense of self-efficacy but who does not wish to change. Helen believes she can make changes if she wishes to, but just cannot see the point because the changed outcome (improved oral health) is of no added personal value to her (or so she believes).

What treatment will you offer to the patient and how will you proceed with the consultation?

Consider particularly:

- Negotiation of a treatment plan that will suit both your ethics and the patient's wishes

- The patient's 'beliefs' regarding her diet and her future oral health

- What key motivations to health and oral health are important to this patient?

Case Three

Richard is a 37-year-old Marketing Director, for a small engineering firm. He has three children aged 1, 4 and 7 years. His wife runs the home. He is widely known and liked in the small community in which your practice is located. He travels widely with his work. He has been a regular dental attender all his life and has no symptoms at present. He claims to brush his teeth twice a day and says he is attending to ensure that no problems will occur in the future.

On examination, you discover that the upper lateral incisors are both missing, having been removed when the patient was a child due, he says, to 'having too many teeth'. The four first permanent molars are also missing, but the remaining posterior teeth have only minimal occlusal restorations. His oral hygiene is excellent and there are no signs of periodontal involvement.

How will you proceed in order to ensure:

- That the patient's current level of oral health is maintained?
- That your practice 'markets' itself to the patient, his family and the local community.

Case Four

Damien is a 17-year-old male. He has attended your practice intermittently for many years. When he was 8, his four first permanent molars were extracted at your practice because of gross caries. The last time you encountered Damien was when he was 13-years-old. The case notes reveal that at that time his oral hygiene had been extremely poor and he had made it clear that he was unlikely to cooperate with any treatment. His mother had accompanied him. He has now attended at your practice, asking you to "check that everything's okay". On examination, it is noted that Damien's oral hygiene is now fair/good, he has 'white spot', carious lesions on his upper lateral incisors and radiographs reveal that he has enamel caries on the approximal surfaces of two posterior teeth, and caries which apparently penetrates to the enamel-dentine junction on one other approximal surface.

Damien's history reveals that he now has a girl friend (of whom he shows you a picture), that he 'trains' regularly at a gym, and that he consumes three to four cans of 'sports drinks' per day. He claims to brush regularly, but complains that he has a 'bad taste' in his mouth when he wakes up in the morning.

How would you proceed with Damien?

Consider particularly:

- Why Damien has attended your practice at this time
- The relationship between his caries and his 'problem'
- What treatment you would offer to Damien?

Case History 1 – One approach

Sandra is a particularly interesting case. She is demanding treatment under general anaesthesia and appears to wish you to take complete responsibility for her oral health. The first question that Sandra raises is whether you should accede to her wishes and arrange for dental treatment to be carried out under general anaesthesia?

In order to answer this question, it is necessary to consider carefully: firstly, what Sandra's 'problem' with her teeth is, which has prompted the visit; secondly, why and how she felt able to combat her 'phobia' and enter the practice; thirdly, what effect her social and personal history might have on the 'success' of any treatment, and fourthly the root cause of her 'phobia' (not necessarily in this order).

Consider the personal history carefully. Put yourself in the patient's shoes.

How would you feel, singing to an audience with a denture that replaced teeth in the anterior portion of your mouth? Consider how important the nightclub spots are to Sandra. They supplement her income and she clearly leaves her daughter in order to do this job. She is not currently in pain and therefore it would seem that the singing career has a lot to do with why she wishes to have treatment. For anyone who performs to an audience, appearance is important. For someone who sings, an ability to articulate clearly is also vital. Thus, although Sandra has not attended for dental care for years, her occupation has prompted the visit. This case is a fine example of the relevance of personal history, e.g. occupation, to appropriate treatment planning and patient satisfaction.

Consider next Sandra's past lifestyle. The domestic violence is important. From your point of view, it has caused great damage to the patient's oral health. Perhaps to Sandra, it also indicates that her health is not under her control, it is under the influence of dramatic, and to her, uncontrollable events. How would this event affect Sandra's trust in people, and in particular in males? Furthermore, the incident during the extraction of an apparently un-anaesthetised tooth must have had a great deal to do with Sandra's mistrust of dentists. Again, imagine the situation. Imagine that you are in such distress/pain that you cannot cope. Then the individual in whom you have placed your trust tells you that the pain you are feeling is not 'real'. Whether Sandra's tooth was or was not properly anaesthetised is immaterial. Only the patient knows how she feels. To continue to extract a tooth when a patient has declared that she cannot continue with the procedure, is as much an 'assault' as was the domestic violence to which this patient had been subjected. If you think about this scenario, it is understandable that Sandra believes that the only acceptable way to receive dental treatment is to be asleep. If we are to expect patients to hand control over, to the extent that we, rather than they, decide what is painful, and which procedures are acceptable, perhaps the only solution is for them to be unconscious! Sandra no longer believes that mutual participation between dentist and patient, during treatment, is possible. She therefore wishes to abdicate all responsibility and control, but the only way she thinks she can do this is via a general anaesthetic.

The dental history is also important, particularly the heavily restored posterior teeth. This evidence of successful treatment shows that the patient has in the past coped with fairly lengthy dental procedures. Thus, the source of Sandra's phobia seems to be clear.

From the above, it should be clear that this patient's 'locus of control' was completely external. She had been subjected to violence from partners, had been allowed no control in a previous dental procedure, she had had an unplanned pregnancy. In general, she could be forgiven for believing that life is a series of random, and often unfortunate events, rather than something over which she has any control.

And so, the objectives of the treatment plan. The team involved believed that the ultimate objective with this patient was to try to enhance Sandra's health locus of control, and sense of self-efficacy. Firstly, by asking Sandra about the restorations in her mouth, we were able to point out to her that she was able to cope well with treatment, if it was carried out by someone she trusted. Secondly, Sandra's success in carrying out oral hygiene practices was highlighted. Analogies with similar people who had NOT done so well were drawn, in order that Sandra could feel that she could succeed in controlling her oral health, because she was more able than others. Again, this work was done by the dental nurse, who had been able to strike up a much greater rapport with Sandra than the dentist.

The team in this case felt that the worst possible plan would be to give Sandra a general anaesthetic. It was agreed that, since the patient was not, at the time, in pain, the objective would be initially to gain the patient's trust and encourage her to understand that the team could help, but only if she wished this to happen. This was followed by an agreement, a sort of 'cooling-off period' in which the team were to decide what they could offer, and she was to decide whether she wished to embark on treatment. A date was agreed on which Sandra was to ring to arrange to come for a 'chat', during which the treatment options would be explained to her, and having listened to these she would then have two weeks to decide on the plan that she preferred.

Sandra has now had the upper right central and lateral incisors successfully root-treated and re-restored. A new denture has been provided, with the option of a bridge being available at a later date.

Case History 2 – One approach

Here, you have been asked how you would negotiate a treatment plan that will suit both you, and the patient. Before you can answer this, let us first dissect out the components that are important to each of the participants in this negotiation.

Firstly, what of Helen's health habits? On questioning, Helen is evidently intelligent and articulate. She is well-educated and knows the relevant facts about the links between smoking and health and the links between sugar consumption and dental decay. Lack of knowledge is therefore not a problem in this case. She regards her teeth as things that, if they break down, she simply attends the dentist to have them repaired. Cost is not a problem and Helen is unconcerned by treatment. Therefore, she sees no need whatsoever to alter her behaviour because the 'health' of her teeth is not of any consequence. Her only concern, and the reason for her visit, is the appearance of her teeth and mouth. She regards her teeth more as a fashion accessory than a health concern.

What of Helen's wishes? She wants you to place a gold pontic to fill the gap caused by the missing upper left first premolar. Can you ethically agree to do this? Your professional knowledge tells you that a bridge placed in someone with such a high caries rate is likely to fail very rapidly. Also, will it be helpful or harmful to Helen's incipient periodontal problems to fit a bridge? She is clearly susceptible to periodontal disease.

Helen is the type of patient who knows what she wants and expects it to be provided. What is likely to happen if you insist on a preventive regime rather than providing the bridge? Well, what will happen is that Helen will simply go to another practice until someone will give her what she wants.

It is apparent that appearance is the key to any change in Helen's habits. She listened with interest to descriptions of 30-year-old women whose looks had been compromised by having to have crowns fitted on anterior teeth. She was also very keen to know more about 'getting long in the tooth'. However, it was also clear that this was not going to change the patient's dietary habits, so the dilemma remained about which treatment plan might be appropriate.

The outcome was that, in return for a written promise that Helen would attend regularly for the upkeep of her rapidly decaying teeth, it was agreed to provide a bridge. It was also explained (and written down) that the bridge would be very unlikely to have an extended lifespan if Helen's diet remained unchanged. She accepted this and signed the 'disclaimer'.

Thus, the dental team's conscience was clear and Helen was not disappointed by a refusal to provide what she wanted.

As stated in Chapter 5, sometimes the answer to exhortations to change for the sake of one's health is 'no'. Sometimes patients simply do not want to take action for the sake of their health. So long as the dental team are certain that the right information in an appropriate form has been given, there is little else they can do. In Helen's case, 'prevention' would have to take the form of regular and early treatment of disease, rather than primary prevention and it was agreed that a promise of regular attendance represented the best solution.

Case History 3 – One approach

After one glance at this case, any practitioner who is 'practice building' will want this patient to attend his/her surgery. The patient is motivated, healthy, has three children who are likely to be healthy but who may have a need for orthodontic treatment. The individual is also respected, liked and well-known in the local community and knows about marketing. This chap is a dream patient!

Again, consider the patient's lifestyle. He comes from a quite amazingly 'traditional' type of family. This is important to note, for a number of reasons. Firstly, people with traditional views tend to have a somewhat old-fashioned view of dentists and dental treatment. Although very willing and conforming, Richard might find it difficult to participate fully in treatment decisions. He will 'do as he is told' without question, but a considerable amount of work will be required in order to encourage Richard to feel that he can take part in his dental treatment. Secondly, it would be a waste of time to try to influence Richard's oral hygiene habits, particularly his use of products such as paste, floss, brushes, etc., as clearly such things are organised and run by his wife. Indeed, Richard's appointment was made by his wife, as he was about to go on a trip abroad.

With regard to marketing your practice to this patient: firstly, he should be congratulated on having maintained his mouth to such a high standard. Secondly, and much more importantly, Richard is a staunch family man. His family and his job are the two great interests in his life and he adores his children. Enquiring about his children and inviting them along to the practice with their Mum, would be very important. Furthermore, if Richard is to have a course of treatment, the simple measure of remembering (making a note of) his children's names, and someone (? receptionist) asking about them when he returns to the practice, will let him know that both he, and his family, are of interest and concern. If this is done, it is unlikely that Richard will ever attend any other practice. Here, once again, it is evident that simple courtesies and considerations for patients' feelings by all members of the team can act as powerful practice building tools.

Richard would also be likely to market your practice to the community. He is known and liked, and knows about marketing. He has three children who all have contemporaries and will need dentists. Patients like Richard are rare and can be very valuable to a practice. Make sure you don't lose opportunities!

Case History 4 – One approach

Damien is a typical adolescent. He has clearly switched from his teenage rebelliousness (*vis-a-vis* his oral hygiene and non-cooperation during his visit four years ago) to a wish to act as an independent adult. His new girl friend is clearly very important to him and has probably acted directly, or indirectly, as a stimulus to the current visit. He has dramatically improved his oral hygiene, but his white spot lesions would suggest that this is a recent change in behaviour. Like most teenagers, Damien is very body/ appearance conscious. On questioning about the gym, Damien revealed a pride in his appearance, in his sense of health, and in his ability to stick to his training programme. Here you have a golden opportunity to bring Damien's high self-efficacy and health locus of control to his attention, and then extend the praise to include his oral health. This places his oral health into a context that is highly relevant to Damien. He must recognise that his mouth is part of his body, which is becoming increasingly important to him.

Damien is complaining that he has a bad taste in his mouth in the mornings. Further questioning revealed that this was not the exact problem. Damien's real worry was that his breath might smell less than fresh first thing in the morning. The connection between this new concern and the fact that he has a new girl friend can only be speculated on!

The examination has revealed early caries in Damien's mouth. Firstly, although Damien should be informed of your findings, he must be reassured that this early decay has nothing whatever to do with his morning halitosis. You would also need to offer advice about his complaint, brushing, avoiding hunger, avoiding strong and spicy foods, avoiding alcohol, drinking water, etc.

In terms of treatment, Damien is a problem. All of his problems are on the borderline of treatment need, i.e. they are things that 'could' rather than 'should' be treated. If you were to tell Damien that he's fine and to come back in a year, he will probably assume that since he has existed in 'health' for the last four years without attending, he will probably be able to exist for another four. If, on the other hand, you were to restore all the approximal lesions, you are externalising the patient's newly found internal health locus of control, which is the opposite of what you want to happen. Really, Damien needs to be advised regarding the non-healthy aspects of the 'sports' drinks and allowed to control his own oral health. A fluoride rinse might also be helpful.

Damien is at an important stage. Action is required now if his newfound interest in his body and its workings is to be harnessed for the benefit of his oral health.